Copyright Notice

No part of this book may be reproduced or transmitted in any form whatsoever, electronic, or mechanical, including photocopying, recording, or by any information storage or retrieval system without expressed written, dated and signed permission from the author. All copyrights are reserved.

Disclaimer

Reasonable care has been taken to ensure that the information presented in this book is accurate. However, the reader should understand that the information provided does not constitute legal, medical or professional advice of any kind.

No Liability: this product is supplied "as is" and without warranties. All warranties, express or implied, are hereby disclaimed. Use of this product constitutes acceptance of the "No Liability" policy. If you do not agree with this policy, you are not permitted to use or distribute this product.

We shall not be liable for any losses or damages whatsoever (including, without limitation, consequential loss or damage) directly or indirectly arising from the use of this product.

Accelerated Learning:

Learn 10x Faster, Improve Memory, Speed Reading, Boost Productivity & Transform Yourself Into A Super Learner

The 11 Craziest Predictions About the Future Experts Say Are Going to Happen

Here are 11 predictions about the future that may surprise or even shock you—but one thing is certain: They're backed by some pretty smart people.

Find Out Now

Accelerated Learning & Memory Improvement To Learn Faster, Improve Your Memory & Save Time Even If You Have a Bad Memory Or Are Easily Distracted

Table of Contents

Introduction

Chapter One: How we learn
- Experiential Learning
- Observational Learning
- Associative Learning
- Activity-based learning
- Intentional self-learning

Chapter Two: Building Concentration

Chapter Three: The Concept of Time And Best Conditions For Learning

Chapter Four: The Importance Of Mentors
- What is a mentoring relationship?
- How to seek out a mentor in your chosen field
- The qualities of a good mentor
- How can a mentor help you learn faster?

Chapter Five: The Connection Between Your Habits And Learning Process
- Identify unproductive habits
- Build organizational skills
- Self-discipline and will power
- Deliberately chose to set a good example
- Habits that stretch your goals
- Build a growth mindset

Chapter Six: Developing Speed Reading Skills

Chapter Seven: Photographic Memory

Chapter Eight: The Concept Of Self Improvement

Identify with a vision for your life
Keep your eyes on the future

Conclusion

Introduction

Life is evolutionary!

We are living in times when things change sporadically, and if we are not proactive with these changes, we will be left behind. The best way to become a part of 'life's strategic evolution is to seek ways to learn faster!

In today's world, the person who doesn't learn with speed loses out and becomes unaware of what life entails. Such persons may say they rely on their experiences. But the truth is in the race of life; your expertise is only as vital with how valuable it is in helping you solve complex issues.

So we have established the premise that learning is compulsory, but that fact is at the base level, and this book is all about taking things up a notch. To go beyond the basics in life, you must look beyond the average learning rate to considering the development and retention of knowledge at the speed of light

The answer? Accelerated Learning!

Accelerated learning is a form of teaching and learning which enables learners to go beyond limiting beliefs and misconceptions while tapping into their hidden potential.

With accelerated learning, participants gain access to a multidimensional learning approach. This approach enables them to retain information in a multisensory and natural way.

When you think about accelerated learning, think about a natural way for people to learn anything that encompasses the emotional, intellectual, and physical aspects of their lives. The learner receives a holistic training process that leads to a build-up of effective yet fast learning processes.

Accelerated learning was introduced to the world by Dr. Georgi Lozanov, who used to teach about 60 students using a variety of non-traditional techniques. These techniques included the use of visual and auditory methods termed as "Innovative learning."

Dr. Lozanov wanted the students to learn faster, and he had tremendous results to show for his efforts. Over the years, several academics, professionals, and researchers developed his idea further. Today, accelerated learning is a cost-effective yet impactful way of utilizing the brain.

People who struggle in school, workplaces, and everywhere else they are required to use their brainpower feel trapped in their minds. These persons know that they are smart but are unable to translate that feeling into what they do.

Accelerated learning gives them a platform to re-learn how to learn, double their reading speed, and increased ability to remember anything. The results of accelerated learning can completely change the trajectory of your life while repositioning you for a successful life evolutionary process.

This book aims to empower you through accelerated learning to get the most out of your learning experience so you can excel at whatever you wish to do in life.

Through the pages, chapters, and sections of this book, you will unearth some of the most enthralling accelerated learning techniques. The tools you will discover will help you gain mastery over anything you wish to learn.

If you are eager to learn faster, conquer your challenges, and get more out of life, you are reading the right book!

Chapter One: How we learn

There are a hundred billion neurons or brain cells in our brain. Whenever we learn, new information passes through synapses along pathways.

The process of learning occurs when we create and strengthen the pathways in our brain based on input. While all of our minds can absorb Information faster through education, not everyone is keen on intentionally developing that aspect of the brain.

We all have varying learning capacities based on our level of motivation, our personality, learning styles, and an awareness of our learning process.

However, to gain a balanced learning experience, we must become aware of our learning process.

The most beautiful concept about life is the fact that we learn daily consciously or unconsciously. What have you been doing today? (Please note we will be asking a lot of questions as it will help you get the most out of this book in terms of implementation).

So let's go back to the question: what did you do today? Did you stay at home? Go to the office? Spent time with friends? Even if your day is still ongoing, you will agree that at some point, you learned something in the course of your daily experience.

Now some people are very conscious of their learning patterns, so it is easier for them to know when they've discovered something. On the other hand, some learn without being aware of it. But as they live on, they apply what they learn through their decisions.

This book will help you to be conscious of your learning process and gain insight into viable ways through which you can accelerate that process.

But for us to achieve this objective, we must start on the basis, like kids who are just learning the alphabet at school. We can't dive directly into accelerated learning without first knowing the foundational aspects of learning.

If your doctor recommended that you eat more fruit, you would want to know WHY before you ask HOW. The ability to see the reason why we do whatever we do is what makes us intelligent human beings.

So before we get to subsequent chapters that are replete with steps you can take towards imbibing accelerated learning, you must first understand elementary concepts.

Which brings us to the initial statement and title of the chapter "How we learn."

Experiential Learning

Experiential learning is one of the most intriguing learning processes. It is fascinating because we experience things every second, from feelings to events, and in this pool of experiences, we draw out lessons that become a part of our lives.

If a baby touches the flames on a candle even for a brief second, he/she will experience a painful, fiery sensation. The sensation will cause him/her to stay far away from a candle the next time he/she sees a one (even years later).

That baby has gained experiential knowledge!

Experiential is from the word "Experience," and it is all about how you learn from what happens to you. Now, sometimes we control our experiences and some other times we don't. But the point is that so long you experience something you will most likely learn from it (positive or negative).

There will be times when you experience something and still won't learn anything from it not because there is no lesson to be discovered. But because you are unconscious of experiential learning.

Have you ever heard the statement "There is a silver lining in every cloud?" well that statement speaks of the impact of experiential learning. Life will be so much easier for you, and you will achieve your goals faster when you are conscious of learning through your experiences.

Even if something negative happened to you, maybe you lost your job or got involved in an accident. After your initial reaction, if you scrutinize the situation, you will find a lesson from that experience.

Guess what? The next job you get, you will be mindful of the lessons you gained in the previous one, thus adding value to your experience. Experiential learning is also the oldest learning process.

Back in the olden days when agriculture was the only means of financial empowerment for men and women, farmers relied on experiential knowledge. Those farmers gained insight into the state of crops and planting seasons through experience.

So the results they get using a specific method in a particular time determines if they will continue with that method or not. But over the years, experiential knowledge developed into a useful guide for living.
First, you immerse yourself in an experience, then you reflect on that experience and gain new ways of thinking or patterns or doing things from your reflection.

It will be impossible to gain insight into an experience without reflecting on it. It is a reflection that helps your mind put the situation in the spotlight and examines every aspect of it.

So you went out with friends to a restaurant, you all got back home and texted each other, agreeing not to return to the restaurant. If you take a little time to reflect on your evening at the restaurant, you will be able to spot the reasons why you didn't have a good evening.

Maybe it was the food, the ambiance, or the waiter. Reflection becomes your ability to gain something meaningful from that experience. Even in the academic world, experiential learning holds sway.

If students take the time to reflect on their past performance at the start of a new semester, they will be able to achieve more. Just by knowing the areas they need to work on, they can score better grades.

Experiential learning is the future of education, and one of the critical reasons for this postulation is the fact that it accelerates the learning process.

Experiential learning entails critical thinking, problem-solving, and decision making, all of which are at the core of accelerated learning. You will find that your level of engagement increases as you can figure out situations, activities, and events quickly because you are involved in the process.

Why are you reading this book? It is because we've found a way for you to learn anything faster. If you understand the concept of experiential learning, then you are halfway through the process.

Experiential learning also means personalized learning: until something happens to you, it might still feel unreal knowing it happened to someone else. This learning process enables you to embrace your journey through life, helping you remain aware of what is going on around you.

Observational Learning

What did you notice about the neighborhood the first time you stepped out of your car into your new home? If you are a person who is keen on the observation of places, you may have noticed a pattern with your new neighbors. You may see how they keep their lawn tidy and beautiful with flowers.

So now you've finally settled into this new home, and every morning you look out the window the flowers register in your mind. You are thinking about creating a garden in front of your home.

Do you know what just happened to you?

It is an observational learning!

You have learned and possibly embraced the idea of a garden solely based on what you observed. Observational learning is quick, sharp, and happens swiftly.

Associative learning takes time. But observational learning is instant. It is as immediate as you being on a bus with someone else for a few hours and imbibing what you observe about the person (positive or negative).

Now you are thinking about planting a garden just because you noticed a peculiar trend in your environment. When someone new moves in and sees your garden, the same thing happens.

So it is safe to say that observational learning creates a ripple effect for people, but it has a similar caveat like some of the other learning patterns.

Not everyone practices observational learning. For you to use this method, you must be fully conscious of what is going on around you.

Someone else may move into the same neighborhood and not notice the gardens. They may settle in for a long time before they observe, and even then, they may decide not to do anything about their lawn.

So you see that although observational learning is instant, you need to observe your environment and the people around you to learn from them.

A lack of awareness in people concerning observation is one of the reasons why accelerated learning is very crucial. When we start the process of teaching you about accelerated learning, you will get to know the crucial role of awareness in a fast learning pattern.

When you are aware, your senses pick up signals from the activities of others, and you can imbibe what they do without getting a direct lecture for them.

But aside from awareness, you must also have a prompt and willing disposition to implement what you learn. Think about this; we are in an era where there is so much conversation about how we can have a cleaner environment.

If you see someone who deliberately picks off dirt by the roadside, you will either learn from him/her by also doing the same. So whenever you see dirt or ignore trash by the roadside, you get it out.

Observational learning takes place when you emulate that person by also contributing to the "Cleaner World." If you don't take action after watching that person for a while, then observational learning has not taken place.

So there are two extremes you must be mindful of:

The first entails being able to observe something or a person.

The second is implementing what you saw.

You may ask, "What if I am not patient enough to observe a person's pattern?" Well, the truth is that we all are not created to pay extra attention to detail.

But the fact that we are not born that way shouldn't hinder us from learning how to be that way. Some persons have that sixth sense they can step into a room and notice the color palette of the walls and furnishings.

If you are not like such a person, then from today you can learn how to pay close attention to everyone and everything you encounter. Being able to do what you were not "Born with" with regards, learning is one of the vital principles of accelerated learning.

You get to realize that we are not born complete, we can complete ourselves by being intentional about filling whatever knowledge gap we have. Look forward to the section on intentional self-learning, it will help you gain further insight into this idea.

Associative Learning

Before we proceed with this learning concept, you should know that the term "Associative learning" has a diverse meaning. The most prominent purpose is of a person or animal learning the association between two stimuli.

The above meaning of associative learning is fantastic. But we are considering associative learning from a different lens. Associative learning within the concept of accelerated learning speaks of the impact we have on each other.

If you have a particular friend, you chat with daily, and this friend communicates with you using specific vocabulary. Eventually, you will find that you talk with other people using the same vocabulary.

You wouldn't know that you are imbibing your friend's vocabulary until someone you chat wit, mentions it out to you. This chat scenario is an example of associative learning.

Associative learning within this context speaks of the kind of learning process you experience through the type of people you associate with or the people you have around you most of the time.

This learning process happens when we spend quality time with a person. Then we slowly absorb his/her mannerisms, making them a part of our conversational styles or life's choices.

Associative learning also takes place when someone has a massive influence over us; this happens mainly between someone who is of a higher cadre and a subordinate.

So when you work closely with your boss at the office, you subconsciously take action based on what you glean from your boss. If your boss insists on using the scanner in a specific way, you will learn to do the same over time.

Associative learning cannot be measured. It is mostly subconsciously achieved. It will be challenging to ascertain the exact time you started gleaning the lessons from the person.

More so, associative learning can go on for a protracted period even after you are no longer in contact with the person; the effect of knowledge continues.

You will find that the lessons learned from this person stay with you and form a vital aspect of your life. Associative learning doesn't happen quickly, unlike other forms of knowledge.

Spending time with a person on a train ride for an hour will cause you to pick some traits of his/her personality. This scenario means you are practicing observational learning. But with associative learning, you are near this individual for some time repeatedly.

More so, the person may not be aware of the fact that you are gleaning something from him/her. While they are just themselves, you are picking up traits and reshaping your life with what you learn from them.

Excitedly. You can also be a source of associative learning for someone else, which is the reason why you must always portray good qualities. Like they say, "You never know who is watching."

One of the most striking futuristic features of this form of learning is the fact that we can help each other. If everyone becomes aware of the power they have over others through associative learning, they will be proactive with doing the right things.

Those who perpetrate evil acts in the world have spent time with others who do the same, which is why some of them do not feel remorseful afterward. They have gained belief systems fully entrenched in their mindset.

Before a person can change his/her lifestyle choices gained through association, he/she has first to become aware. The awareness that there is a problem through an unconscious learning process has to be there. Otherwise, there will be no hope for change!

So while focusing on the positives with associative learning, we should also be mindful of the negative impact it has on the person who is gleaning from another individual with the "Wrong" values.

The power of associative learning is one of the primary reasons why parents are advised to keep a keen eye on the kind of friends around their kids.

Activity-based learning

Based on recent statistics, most people say they achieve more with activity-based education because it keeps them active and very involved in the process.

Kids and adults love the thrill of activities when they learn for varying reasons. For some persons, exercises keep them grounded in a way that they can complete tasks and remain committed to the process long-term.

Let's go back to the first time you learned how to prepare a meal, depending on who taught you or if you were self-taught as we will learn shortly. You will agree that it wouldn't have been possible for you to learn without actually cooking.

Armed with the recipes you want to utilize, you visit the farmers market, and commence cooking. While cooking, you will observe some disparities between the content of the process and your actual meal.

You will also realize that you don't have to stick to the recipe word for word as you can become creative with the cooking process. All of this new knowledge you gain while carrying out the cooking activity is the beauty of this type of learning.

Even in schools, if you visit a typical art class in an elementary school, you will see first-hand the dynamism with activity-based learning. For example, kids shown a picture of a green lizard, are told to draw theirs and paint it using their green crayons.

After the exercise, when you go through their artworks, you will find that the idea of the color "Green" isn't unilateral. Every child will have their interpretation of what the lizard in the picture looks like and the color green.

However, when we hear activity-based learning most of the time, our minds think about children learning because it is a vital part of the school's curriculum.

It goes beyond that because of all the learning processes, activity-based learning is the one we all need and practice. Regardless of the number of maternity books read, a new mom has to face the reality of raising a baby. She has to give her baby a bath, feed him/her, change diapers, and do every other thing for the baby.

Now if this new mum solely focuses on the theoretical aspect of motherhood (reading books and listening to podcasts), when the baby arrives, she will be stuck.

So it is safe to say that activity-based learning is the bridge between theory and action. Everything you glean from the other types of education solidified with this learning process.

Putting in the work and implementing what you learn is done through activity-based education. Honestly, it is when you use what you learn that you can authenticate the integrity of the process.

Think about all the ideas you read about in the past but didn't use it. Do you think you would have had a much better experience with your life in general?

Activity-based learning also enables a person to filter information. There is so much information on almost every subject out there today that taking action is the only way to know what works.

With this book, you will be at the theoretical side of knowledge, discovering how to implement the concept of accelerated learning. But the only way to ascertain if you can genuinely learn things faster is to bring the words in this book to life through activity-based education.

By taking the suggestions, ideas, and steps, you will discover and apply them in your daily activities. While at work, at home or wherever you will be completing the learning process.

Activity-based learning also serves as a confidence booster. The only reason you will volunteer to prepare all the meals for the next family event is that you have perfected your cooking skills through persistent practice.

So you will be doing a lot of activity-based learning after reading this book entirely. Only this time, you will apply more speed and gain more within a short time.

Intentional self-learning

Another meaningful way we learn is through the deliberate self-learning process. Now, this learning process is placed last in this section because it is an idea that entails a person being conscious of their learning patterns. Although, fewer people who take this learning route.

There are two keywords to note there:

1. *Intentional*
2. *Self-learning*

Being intentional is akin to being consciously aware that you need to do something and go for it. Sometimes we learn because we "Have" to and not because we "Need" to.

Learning because you have to cause you to discover new things because you have an obligation to, maybe you are in school or your workplace. In such environments, you do not have the choice to either be intentional unintentional.

On the other hand, learning because you need to compels you to become intentional. It is this kind of learning process that makes you go online to seek answers to questions on YOUR OWN.

But there is a process for this kind of learning, and again it has to do with being aware.

First, you become aware of the fact that you've got a gap in knowledge, maybe you are out with friends, and everyone knows how something works, but you don't. Instead of brushing it aside, you take on the adventurous tasks of learning.

But with this process, you don't need a teacher because you are self-motivated. It is probably something you can teach yourself in this technologically advanced age.

Intentional self-learning is a fantastic way of adding value to your life because there is no limit to what you can learn. The only obstruction to this kind of learning is awareness, and this begs the question, "Are you aware of what you know and what you don't know?"

A person can live for a long time and still need help with a lot of basic things because all through their lives, they were never aware of what they lacked or the void in their knowledge space.

So while their peers execute a lot of things on their own, they relied on someone else. When such persons grow older, they have to be around other people regularly to get things done.

The purpose of learning is growth!

The growth that enables you to become independent because you know how things work. Intentional self-learning also applies to some kids raised in homes where they are taught to question everything.

A child who is raised to ask questions consistently will become proactive with seeking out ways to gain knowledge for himself/herself. It could be learning how to arrange the wardrobe or how to use a bedsheet on the bed.

Children can also intentionally learn when they are in school without the help of a teacher. The stimulation from the classroom will enable them to use their imagination for educational purposes.

Intentional self-learning happens every day; it is the reason online search engines are crucial to our modern-day living existence. You wouldn't have to ask anyone else a question when you can request a search engine. Get answers, steps, and detailed information on how to learn a new concept.

The individual's level of motivation primarily determines the success rate with intentional self-learning. This situation means that if you are highly motivated, you will not only be able to learn, you will be inspired to share what you discovered.

The motivational factor will also cause you to seek other ways of learning similar ideas to what you initially set out to gain. So let's return to the child who uses this process.

When he self-learns how to make his/her bed, the first attempt may not be significant. The edges of the bedsheet might not have been well-tucked in, so he/she is motivated to have perfect tips.

Then the child feels a sense of accomplishment; he/she runs off to the adult in the house to showcase the results of his intentional self-learning. Upon receiving a high-five or a pat on the back for a job well done, the child doesn't stop learning.

Instead, he is motivated to take on several other tasks, and this is the most profound benefit of intentional self-learning: it never ends! With the right level of motivation, a person can gain so much knowledge such that there will be little or no gaps in his/her learning process.

But all of this information on the various ways we learn still borders on the status quo, on what was and is still obtainable. We can do better with learning; we can go faster!

What we have achieved with this first chapter is to lay the groundwork and foundation for the other concepts we will discuss. But knowing how we learn isn't enough, it's a good start, but it isn't enough. We need to discover how to learn faster so we can achieve much more.

We will begin with a vital part of accelerated learning: Concentration!

*Avoid putting yourself under pressure to learn using all methods. This chapter isn't a prescriptive one. We are merely presenting the ways people learn, so you are conversant with each process.

Chapter Two: Building Concentration

Elephant! (Read on, we will come back to this word).

You have received insight into the concept of how we learn. Which serves as a foundation, but there is more to discover. Beginning with this chapter, we will be sharing more insight into how you can utilize accelerated learning. You will find how to learn anything faster than your current ability using concentration skills.

The first step towards accelerated learning is to build concentration!

You should know that the first time you learn something new can be frustrating. The frustration is common for everyone else; you are not alone with this challenge. This feeling of inadequacy is the reason why accelerated learning is vital in helping you get over that feeling of frustration from the start.

If you want to learn anything or do the things you do currently at a faster rate, you must have the ability to concentrate fully on the task. But some things get in the way of concentration all the time; we call them distractions.

On an average day, you deal with over 34 gigabytes of information from your home, to the office and every other activity you do in the day. Every 11 minutes, your work or task is interrupted, and for you to get back to the job, it will take an additional 25 minutes.

The statistics above means that our ability to focus is dwindling daily with external and internal distractions. But if you can master the art of concentration, then your internal and external world will be constructed appropriately.

Your mind cannot work in chaos, and since your senses are prone to distraction quickly, you need to work on refocusing your mind. You can redirect your attention by bringing it back to the task at hand.

Concentration means taking your mind off several things and maintaining focus on one thing at a time. It is the base of accelerated learning; the one aspect of knowledge you must be proficient in else every other issue will be affected. You cannot relate well with your mentor if you cannot concentrate, you will struggle with your use of time if you cannot focus.

So it truly all begins with concentration. When you conquer building this important learning technique, every other thing falls into place. Your attention is crucial if you want to learn fast.

However, you should know that improving your concentration level takes time and requires a lot of practice, but the result is always worth it. After gaining the edge with concentration, you will realize that your brain is super active and you can execute arduous tasks with ease.

Now let's go back to the word at the beginning of the chapter "Elephant," did you think about an elephant when you read that word? Did you see an elephant in your mind while reading through the section? Are you distracted by the thought of an elephant?

If you answer honestly, you will say that you did think about an elephant and even right now, the thought of an elephant reigns supreme in your mind.

Why are we talking about an elephant now?

You see, that is the power of distraction over the human mind. This book is not even about animals, yet you are thinking about an animal. You are thinking about it because you read a word at the start of this chapter.

A single word can shatter your concentration, and this is the reason why you are unable to complete tasks on time. Distraction is also the reason why you get involved with other time-draining activities such as procrastination.

It is difficult today to maintain focus than in the past. Today, so many things compete for your attention. You've got kids, social media, bills to pay, nosy/noisy neighbors, conversations you have with yourself; it is an unending list.

But when you learn how to take control of your mind through the process of building concentration, you will be able to carry out tasks swiftly. You will also experience reduced stress, and you will be happier with yourself.

So to the question you are asking right now: how do I build concentration? Well let's find out, shall we?

1. Know yourself

The first step to take towards building concentration is self-awareness! We are keen on helping you get to the base of this aspect of learning. It is when you are self-aware, you will be able to identify your concentration lapses and build on them.

So have you been monitoring your concentration levels lately?

What are the environmental triggers that get you easily distracted?

When last did you attempt learning something new?

How quick are you with learning new skills?

You need to have answers to these questions. With solutions, it will be easier for you to know the level of effort you can put into building concentration because we are different people.

Right after this step, we are going to delve into the various ways through which you can build concentration. But if you start utilizing the steps without knowing your weaknesses, you will be applying solutions without understanding the problems.

If you are a mum, maybe the reason you struggle with concentrating on a task or learning new things is that you've got kids around all the time.

If you work in a factory, then your inability to concentrate fully may be attributed to the noise. On the other hand, maybe you are a person who is always easily distracted.

By knowing all of these details, you will know how to tailor a solution that fits your peculiar concentration challenge.

So spend some time with yourself getting to know yourself. You will be amazed at the discoveries you unearth. This discovery will be the best step you will take because self-awareness enables you to stay true to who you are while working to become better.

2. **Meditate and Read**

Studies have shown that active meditation for about 5-10 minutes every day aids better concentration. A lot of times, we don't meditate because we ascribe some spiritual ideas to the process, but that isn't the case.
Meditation is all about blocking off everything that may cause a distraction in your mind and keeping you in a state of calmness where you can focus on tasks.

Now with building concentration, you are meant to meditate daily! You can select a time when you will want to do it but try incorporating it into your day.

So what is the connection between meditation and concentration for accelerated learning?

People who struggle to learn things fast for the first time or subsequently actually have an attention span deficit problem. They are unable to keep their attention on a project for a protracted period.

But with meditation, such persons will find that they have access to the essential aspect of concentration: Control.
Accelerated learning is all about control, your ability to control how you learn at a rapid rate. But how are you going to manage your learning pace when you are unable to maintain calm in your mind?

So take a few minutes off every day, shut out everything else, and focus on the rhythm of your breathing. You will find that you have built a stronger attention span that enables you to learn anything fast.

You will transfer the meditative skills to focusing on whatever you want to learn. Now reading is also an essential activity you must engage in to build concentration

To read and understand, you have to sit down and read the content in the book word for word (just like you are doing right now). It takes a lot of discipline to sit still and read through a book.

Reading is for people who are keen on building concentration for accelerated learning long term. Try to maintain the same kind of focus when reading various genres of books and read every day!

As you read, the easier it becomes for you to focus on a new skill and learn faster; this is because reading trains your mind and your brain.

Your ability to strike a connection with the content of the book. Assimilate the material, understand it, and apply it to your life will also become useful in helping you learn anything at a faster pace.

3. Build focused stamina slowly

Meditation puts you in a great place to attain calm when learning something new, and this is great for concentration. However, you should know that building concentration is a process.

We are taking you through the process with all the details in this chapter, and a vital part of that process is building focused stamina slowly.

Everyone has a focus threshold: some people can stay focused on a task for an entire hour successfully while others struggle through 30 minutes. Now even when you have robust focused stamina, please know that you can always build on it.

Before building focus stamina, you need first to measure your level of focus on a task. So how long does it take for you to work on a job? You can use this book to find out the answers.

How long did it take to finish the first chapter? 30 minutes? One hour? Two hours? Were you distracted as you read? Did you read it all word for word?

If you can get the precise time, then you will be able to know how to improve on it. Concentration levels should be equal to knowledgeable input.

So as you concentrate, make sure you are putting in the amount of time you will need to learn the new skill. If you desire to create an app, for example, before getting right to it, discover the duration it will take for you to complete the app.

If the regular timing is six months, you need to divide your time into the months by allotting the number of hours you can put in per day that will enable you to create that app in 2-3 MONTHS (excellently).

That's the purpose of accelerated learning, so you can learn how to do things swiftly and not at the "Normal" pace for you to achieve this, you need to build focus stamina.

Start at where you are by recognizing your current stamina and then using your calculation on how you should attain the desired goal at a shorter time, work towards increasing focus stamina daily.

If at this point you can only focus for five minutes, do great work in those five minutes. Then, the following day, it increases to ten minutes. While you grow, ensure you are getting quality work done, and soon enough, you will realize that you have increased the ability to maintain focus for a longer time.

On the flip side if you struggle with concentration entirely, then we will have to help you with the one minute mark. Select a task you can focus on for one minute alone.

You can try a breathing exercise, work on breathing in and out for 60 seconds without any interruptions. It may seem easy, but many people struggle with focusing on breathing.

If you have challenges with concentration, this simple one-minute breathing exercise will help you build stamina. It is all about taking baby steps until you reach your desired target.

4. Immediately dismiss irrelevant thoughts

Now, this is a serious one!
What is that thing you've always wanted to learn? Take some time to think about this question: do you have an answer now? Great!

So why haven't you taken a step towards learning this skill or whatever it is? Could it be that you didn't try learning it because you were afraid? Are you worried about taking a step? Do you feel like your chances of succeeding with it are slim?

Well, let me say this to you; we all have been there at some point in our lives. You can learn what you desire, you can become an expert in that field, but first, you need to gather your thoughts for better concentration. Irrelevant thoughts show up in our minds twice prominently when we want to learn something new:

The first time we feel them is right before we register for that class or contemplate learning that skill. We start to feel like we have no business going in that direction.

The second time happens when we start to learn, we take the first steps towards learning and midway into it; we experience a freeze.

Now at both times, you need to be proactive with dismissing the thoughts because they are entirely irrelevant. Allowing the ideas to remain in your mind will only make you lose concentration, and you wouldn't act on task.

Self-doubt is a severe problem for people who are keen on breaking free from their comfort zone and learning something new. Some of these people deal with the external issues well enough still struggle with the main challenge: thoughts.

Any thought that settles in your mind telling you that you cannot learn this fantastic new concept fast is irrelevant. Do not entertain the thoughts by contemplating on it or giving it room to fester continually.

Concentration is about awareness, you are aware of what you need to do, and you are committed to it, but at this stage, you shouldn't be solely committed to what you want to learn. Pay attention to what your mind is saying to you as you learn.

Are you getting internal reinforcement? Or are you being put down in your mind? There is a social media term I will introduce at this time. This social media term says, "Be your cheerleader."

You've got to cheer yourself as you peel through the layers of learning.
You want to learn how to fly a plane, for example. When you get to the tarmac, get strapped into the training plane, take a deep breath, and be still for a few seconds.

Then listen to your thoughts!

If you hear negative words, don't take off with that plane until you have changed those negative expressions to positive self-talk. When you succeed at changing your thoughts, you will find that all the apprehension you felt initially ebb away.

At this stage, your first flying practice will go smoothly, and this initial success will inspire you to go faster and harder next time.

5. Sleep is powerful

When you are dealing with your predictable schedule, which entails the regular tasks and things you do daily, you can quickly scale through even when you are tired because you are used to the system.

However, it's challenging when you want to learn something new, something you have never learned before, and you want to do at a fast rate too. So this means that you must prepare mentally and physically.

A lack of proper sleep robs you of your opportunity to achieve accelerated learning. It doesn't matter if you are self-aught or if someone else is teaching you.

If you are not sleeping well enough, you will struggle because a lack of sleep makes your mind less active. You may be physically ready to learn, but you don't feel that way mentally and accelerated learning a program you need to have it all together (physical and mental).

So before you take on this new task, make sure you've slept well, you feel rested and ready to learn. Your mind should be sharp, alert, and quick to receive instructions.

Sleep enables you to feel whole; when you sleep well, you show up to learn with optimism. Even the most challenging task will appear easy to you because, in a rested state, you can achieve anything.

There is never enough emphasis on sleep when we discuss concentration, and this is because some people do not take it seriously. If you want to authenticate this point, try learning something simple (new) when you know you haven't got enough sleep.

Two things will happen:

1. You will feel irritated every time you fail at it

2. You will give up quickly even when you are close to completion.

It wouldn't make any sense to give you all of these fantastic and practical steps on how to activate accelerated learning without offering you the basic idea such as sleep.

Problem solvers realize the importance of sleep, great inventors in the past also acknowledged the role that rest played in helping them get that unique idea.

Yes, you want to learn quickly, oh yes, you are eager to do more now that you have discovered accelerated learning. But without adhering to the recommended sleep hours, you will struggle with this learning pattern.

6. Cut the noise (internal and external)

Another way you can boost your concentration level when learning something new is by cutting off your internal and external noise factors. Now a lot of times we are taught to cut off external noise.

They say, cut out the music or whatever might distract you but what about internal noise? Internal noise consists of your thoughts, musings, and the personal conversations you have within yourself that distract you.

When you have something fundamental to do, you will feel the external distractions that may arise from everything else that happens around you.

When you figure out these external distractions shut them out by taking action. Before commencing work on a project, ensure that everything that will cause you to be distracted is out of the way.

Set your mind on the objective you want to achieve and nothing else until the completion of the project or the set time for whatever you are doing. Which means you must flood your mind with thoughts about the project.

Think about the feeling of satisfaction you will derive from completing the project; allow your mind to wander into the details of the tasks. For example, if you are training to become a fashion designer, for you to create more fashionable pieces at a faster rate, you must think about the finished dress.

Imagine the dress on your favorite muse. Think about the details at the back, the splash of colors, and the fit. You will find consistently renewed energy to complete that dress such that you will finish it in record time. For concentration, when learning how to create, there must be a connection between your mind and the task.

Your mind cannot be fixated on your next vacation when learning how to present a TED talk. The moment your mind strays away from the tasks, you will start to lose concentration and lose time.

When you return to the tasks, you will realize that you've lost so much time and then you give in to what is worse than a distraction: procrastination!
While working on aligning your mind to the task, don't forget to cut off the external noise as well. Always work in an environment that is calm enough for you to execute your projects without distractions.
Now some people say they work better with noise, well, this is the reason we started with the first step, "Know yourself." You've got to know what works for you and stick to it.

But the ultimate goal here is for you to be able to learn new concepts at a faster rate while increasing your speed with older tasks through ACCELERATED learning.

7. Take a break

One reason why you may be finding it very difficult to learn something new is the fact that we get so excited about learning this new concept and we don't take breaks when we get started.

The internet has information on the importance of being disciplined, working hard, motivation, and so many other inspiring contents. All of the inspiration is good, but you cannot learn anything at a fast rate when you are exhausted.

With accelerated learning, you can achieve so much in little time, and it is because you are doing all you can from a position of rest.

If you don't take breaks in-between the learning process, you will feel overwhelmed, and this feeling will cause you to persist, BUT you will be unproductive.

So learning even when you are tired is akin to sitting in a classroom. You can hear the teacher, but you are not paying attention. From the outside people see you in class and say "Oh he/she is learning," but you know within yourself that you are not gaining anything meaningful.

Being able to take breaks is one of the reasons why chapter two is so essential (how to use time). While setting your goals for a particular task, also ensure that you are creating time for breaks.

You will achieve twice as much when you are learning something new after taking a break. You need both the physical and mental breaks. For example, if you want to learn something complex for the first time, you will be introducing a new concept to your brain.

The brain needs time to take in the information you are presenting, so at first, you will get the initial stages right; then it will start to seem complicated. At that point when it looks like t becomes very difficult, take a break!
The fact that you are feeling like it is becoming a challenge means that you are pushing your brain and its ability. So take a few minutes off, take a walk, do something for fun, anything relaxing then come back to the task.

Surprisingly you will find that it is no longer as difficult as it was initially.
So what happened when you took a break? At the time you took a break, you allowed your brain to soak in the information. The mind can create a free flow for the next set of problems you are going to handle.

Develop the habit of taking breaks; you will save time, save energy, and learn faster!

So now you can learn that new language, learn how to bake a cake or do whatever you've always wanted to because you know how to concentrate on a task.

Well done!

You've just completed your first lessons on accelerated learning, which was all about concentration. If you genuinely grasped every detail in this chapter, we can say you can ready for the next experience, which will put your new-found level of attention to the test.

*Please note that dealing with distractions and building concentration isn't an idea you can achieve in one day. Since we all have varying realities, you must settle for what works for you.

Be patient with the process and utilize the steps that work for you!

Chapter Three: The Concept of Time And Best Conditions For Learning

The core of accelerated learning is hinged on time because we are keen on learning things faster, which means we will be taking advantage of the time to learn new things.

If you are going to succeed with accelerated learning, then mastery over time is crucial. But there are also the conditions of learning to consider as even if you know how to utilize time if you are in the wrong learning condition, you will not make much progress.

So think about this chapter like a two-in-one section that helps you achieve the dual concepts of TIME and the right CONDITIONS for learning.

We will begin with time!

Time is the duration in which something happens; it is a resource that is not under the control of anyone as they say, "Time waits for no one." From the moment we gain consciousness, time starts to move, and if you don't own your time, you will never learn anything faster.

Every step we take you through in this book has a connection with the chapters such that your ability to successfully execute the content of a chapter will also inspire you to do the same for the next section.

So we started with concentration because for anyone to gain mastery of time, they need to be able to maintain focus. Now that you have decided to learn using accelerated learning, you must be even more conscious of time.

Now there is an idea that has been quite popular for a while now. The concept speaks of the ability of a person to "Manage" time. We are often told to manage our time well, so we accomplish more in record time.

Well, how do you manage a resource that is entirely out of your control?
The concept of time management cannot hold sway when discussing accelerated learning; we are not going to manage time. Instead, we are going to MAXIMIZE time.

So here is a scenario of the difference between both concepts because you must get this right.
If you were going to learn how to code, for example, when you manage the time you take on the task with the mind-set to do more for as long as you have time.

What this means is that you will resume at your coding table at the regular time (maybe 8 am) and try to do a lot of work from that time till when you are meant to close for the day.

In your mind and the general world perspective, you are managing time; you are doing your best given the amount of time you have. But this also means that you will be unable to learn coding faster because your mind is conditioned to "Manage."

On the other hand, when you maximize the time it doesn't matter if you show up at your coding desk at 8 am or 12 pm, what counts is that even with the few hours you put into coding you will do better, go faster and achieve more because you are getting the best out of your time.

The concept of time management tells you to work for long hours even when you are not making any significant progress; you are to keep working because you want to manage the time.

But when you maximize the time you seek out your PEAK HOURS in a particular period and accomplish even more because at those times you are not conscious of working with time, you are mindful of achieving your goal faster.

Time management is for people with very "Modest" goals; such persons are always conscious of the time, working and waiting for closing hours or when they can stop learning.

Time maximization requires mental toughness and your ability to focus on a goal to accomplish without time restrictions in your head.

To buttress the point we've just made, you will find accelerated learning tips on how to maximize time for a speedy learning experience.

How to maximize time.

1.   *Have a speedy goal*

Do you know why it seemed like you weren't making progress learning swiftly in the past? It was because you didn't have a "Speedy" goal, you had a goal, but not one that suited accelerated learning. Now the game has changed, which means you can no longer have common goals that are aimed at you learning on an average level.

You are no longer managing time. If you are going to maximize your time, you will need goals that inspire you to achieve more without continually looking at the clock.

The fastest runner on earth doesn't practice using the world set records; he practices using the new run time he wants to set. Start thinking like a runner in a race who wants to shatter old records and recreate new ones.

As such, you need first to discover the current record with whatever you are learning. Then set a goal to surpass it. Now the fact that you are going to use a speedy goal doesn't mean you should set an unrealistic one.

That world's best runner knows that he CAN run against a specific time hence the reason for his goal. So if you see that you can surpass the average set goal go for a higher one that doesn't scare but motivate you.

When you start learning using this goal, you will find that you are no longer a time manager because even time cannot hold you down. You now maximize your time as you have a bigger dream ahead of you.

You can write this goal down, place it close to where you learn, so you continuously remind yourself that you must use time wisely to achieve your desires.

2. *Identify your peak hours*

For you to maximize the time you must know your peak hours because all learners are not the same. Now peak hours refer to the times when you are most productive during a specified period (day, week, or month).

For some people, regardless of how seamless the learning process may be, they cannot be useful in early morning hours. So when they learn at such times, they will take some steps but will not be as effective as they would be when learning during peak hours.

Do you know why most elementary schools prefer to teach mental mathematics as the first subject in class in the morning? It is because research has shown that kids do better with mathematics at those times; their minds are fresh and energized for learning.

So you need to find your peculiar peak hours. Using peak hours doesn't also mean you ignore other learning times. What this idea suggests is that you can take on the most challenging aspects of learning that new skill during peak hours as you are guaranteed swift execution.

Now there are some peculiar cases when your peak hours do not suit the recommended time for that particular task. For example, the best time to learn how to play the piano might not be 1 am because the sound of the piano will be a disturbance to those around. So what can you do when your peak hour is 1 am?

Instead of not playing at all, you can use that peak time to learn the theoretical aspects of playing the piano. Then when you get a chance to play the actual keyboard, due to the successful lessons you gained during your peak hours, you will play flawless, now that is how you maximize time!

A person who tries to manage time will want to wait until its morning, well that will mean that the person will also need extra time to learn the theoretical aspects of the class.

Accelerated learning isn't about you learning new things fast at the first try; it means maximizing your time such that you can learn things quicker than others.

You can do twice as much during your peak hours than at your non-peak hours. You will be learning intentionally, with zeal, passion, focus at a time when you are positively and mentally active.

For you to know your peak hours, you will have to study your previous learning patterns. More importantly, you can always improve on your peak hours because now you have a bigger goal to achieve.

3. *Build accountability muscles*

Another way to maximize time as a learning condition while learning something new is building accountability muscles. It is easier for people to set goals than for them to stay accountable to the process.

You will be wasting time by not being accountable because then you wouldn't know how far you have gone and how well you are doing with your goals.

Learning conditions are all about the right environment, tools, and steps you take to ensure you are learning swiftly. But more importantly, you will want to know that you are learning in line with your set goals else you can easily deviate into something else of which the purpose of learning will not be achieved.

With the maximization of time, you've got to check that you are well aligned with your goals regularly. Hence the reason you should build accountability muscles while learning.

When you reach a milestone with your learning process, pat yourself on the back. Then check to ensure the discovery is taking you one step closer to the speedy goal you set initially.

Without accountability, you will move with the tide, like an average learner who has goals but isn't proactive with responsibility. The reason you set goals is to smash them and for direction as well.

Here is a familiar scenario you will love.

There are two people, let's call them Grace and Kelly traveling to another state from the same area. The estimated time for the journey is 5 hours, so they both leave at 1 pm hoping to get there at 6 pm.

Both of them are driving their cars; Grace has a predetermined goal to get to the other state 2 hours before the estimated arrival time while operating within the speed limits.

Grace gets her online map and a physical map (in case there is no network reception). Off she goes, with her goal in mind and driving with all the information she needs.

Kelly, on the other hand, also wishes to get there in record time but has no map. She hopes to ask questions as she goes. So she gets further and stops to ask for directions, she goes a bit further and stops yet again to ask for guidance,

Meanwhile, Grace measures her goal of getting there 2 hours early with her map. Every time she passes a city, she checks the map and is reassured knowing that she is going to hit her target.

That map helps Grace build accountability muscles; she will achieve her goals and use this training with accountability to learn other things.
Grace and Kelly had the same access to time, while one tried to manage it (Kelly) the other maximized it (Grace).

Kelly, on the other hand, did well with setting a goal, but her lack of preparedness made her lose out on being accountable. This scenario applies to everything you seek to learn using the accelerated learning techniques taught in this book. Don't try to manage time; maximize it by being accountable!

4. *Focus on the goal, not the time*

To optimize the time, you need to be conscious of the goals you've set and not the ticking clock else you will be tempted to manage time. Remember that you are using accelerated learning because you want to achieve more and learn faster; hence, your focus shouldn't be on time.

If you narrow down all of your energies into learning using peak hours. While having full concentration, utilizing other ideas shared thus far and subsequently, you wouldn't need to check the clock every minute.

The only thing you need is your goal board with which you practice accountability in checking how far you have gone. With accelerated learning, you have only one goal, and time is a useful resource for you to attain that goal.

So think of time as a resource, you should maximize to get what you want instead of thinking of it as something that is running out quickly.

You don't need more time to learn faster!

You need more centration, focus, dedication, the right learning condition, and every other aspect of accelerated learning to go faster. The way you see time is the way you will use it and monitoring the clock as you learn means you think the time is running out quickly. This mind-set is a temptation for you to manage it.

But when you are productively engaged in the learning process, you wouldn't know when you've been working for over 2 hours or less.

Results are not time-based with accelerated learning. Results are action-based!

5. Avoid time wasters

Can we ever overemphasize this enough? If you've paid close attention to the times you learned in the past, you will agree that from the moment you set your goals, things that will make you waste your time start to creep up on you.

Time wasters are not often glaring; they don't come with a card reading, "I am here to waste your time." Instead, they are familiar with the things we tolerate. Sometimes these are things we do not label frivolous until we start to see the impact they have over the learning experience.

So here it is, whatever will not help advance the course of your goals with learning "At" the time of education is a time-wasting concept. Whoever will not help you gain more insight into the learning process at the time of your learning experience is a time-waster.

There is a slight difference between distractions and time-wasting elements.

When you are distracted, you take your mind off the task for some time, and although it will take a while, you can come back to the duties and still make some progress.

With time-wasting, you lose extended periods because it goes beyond distractions. You stop learning and fixate your attention on this thing or person.

A potential time-waster is a friend you've permitted to drop by at your house or office whenever he/she pleases. Now even when this friend knows that you are seeking knowledge through accelerated learning, he/she will show up at any time to have unproductive discussions.

At the time your friend shows up you are just about reaching a milestone with your learning goals and then you stop! Your friend insists you both grab a meal, you oblige, leave your lesson, and that is how you've wasted time without even knowing it.

If you have tolerated this attitude from your friend for years, you wouldn't see him/her as a time-waster. You wouldn't want to think in that light.
But things have to change.

You cannot be passionate about learning faster and encouraging time wasters. Whether it's a friend, nosy neighbour/colleagues, your kids, parents, etc. you need to stop them in their tracks and reprioritize your life.

Despite the action being more important than time in this context, you still need time. You shouldn't be wasting it with people who are not on the same path as you or will help you in any way.

You can inform time-wasters about your goals and let them know that they cannot show up whenever it pleases them. Inform them that making you do whatever they want you to do is no longer convenient for you.

You can always invite them over or go over to their home/office when you are not learning. You can also completely cut them off if it seems like having the conversation isn't working.

Get to know the value of your learning process and then make a decision based on that when dealing with time wasters.

Conditions for learning

If you know how to maximize your time but do not learn in a conducive environment, you will be doing the right thing in the wrong context.

Where you learn is just as important as how you learn.

We focus so much on learning patterns, tools, and systems while paying little or no attention to the learning condition. So now you've learned how to maximize your time. If you take these lessons and learn in an area where you are easily distracted, you will not achieve your goal.

The dual concepts of time and learning conditions work together (it is the reason the content is in one chapter). If you were to enrol a child in a school for example, even if the school has the best teachers and curriculum, if it is situated directly in front of a factory, you would not go ahead with the admission process.

Your refusal to put your child in that school steams from the fact that the environment is already polluted. Fumes from the factory and the noise it generates are discouraging factors.

Adults like to assume they can manage a learning condition hence the reason they don't pay close attention to this aspect. But the truth is that a poor learning condition may have been the reason why you struggled with learning fast.
Do you know why most people get excited about going back home in the evening after work? It is because there is a feeling that home brings, which expounds on the fact that your environment affects your mental state and learning process.

But learning conditions aren't solely about the environment; it also entails every other part of the learning process that cuts across the availability of the right tools for learning.

So how do you achieve better conditions for learning?

1. *The environment should suit the goal*

If you want to bake the perfect banana bread, where exactly should you be? The bedroom? Or the kitchen? The learning process begins with knowing how you are going to learn, and then where you will learn, which has to be in sync with the goals you are trying to achieve.

A budding tech enthusiast has to be in a room with all the tech gadgets because that is the only way he can make progress while learning. Always make sure your environment blends with what you want to achieve (it's easier to learn faster when you do this).

2. *Get all necessary tools before learning commences*

What is a learning environment without the right tools?

A significant part of learning conditions is having access to tools that will make it easier for you to achieve your goals. But you shouldn't seek out those tools when you start learning; it should before you even commence learning.

Not all learning practices require tools, but if what you are going to learn requires it, make sure you assemble them even if you use them. This step enables you to avoid running off to seek them out when you are at a peak hour.

Getting all of your tools is a sign of preparation for a fantastic accelerated learning experience. When you get the right tools you need before time, it shows your readiness to optimize time not manage it (remember our discourse on this?).

So start with a list of general items you will need and then gradually narrow it all down to the essentials. If you have to buy some brand new items, please do and if you can improvise then go ahead.
The point is that for a better learning condition experience through accelerated learning; you need preparation with everything you require.

3. Learn in a positively-driven environment

You will be the product of your learning environment, so what is it going to be? Positive learning experience? Or a negative one? A learning condition isn't perfect until it entails a positively-driven environment where a learner is inspired to achieve more.

It doesn't matter if you choose to learn at home. If it isn't positively enriching to your learning experience, then you've got a problem. So how do you know you've got a positively-driven environment?

- The environment suits what you are learning. For example, if you are going to learn how to swim, you need to use a well-built swimming pool.

- If you have to learn with other people, then you are surrounded by those who can help you through your creative process.

· In that learning environment, your mind is open to thinking because you are surrounded by stimulating influences.

· A positively-driven climate is one where you feel confident. There are learning environments you step into, and your confidence level drops. Be conscious of how you feel in your learning space; if you don't feel motivated, don't learn there.

Always insist on a positively-driven environment else you will have a lot of energy to put into learning, and the wrong context will zap it all out.

4. *Utilize a vital learning condition: Feedback*

This learning condition is known for years in varying learning sectors, and it still applies to accelerated learning. In the same way, we emphasized the importance of accountability; we are also saying feedback is crucial.

Now if you have a tutor who is teaching you this new idea then insist on getting feedback on your learning strides. Remember that you are working towards a goal, and feedback is the mechanism you need to know if your learning style or pattern will lead you to that goal.

Now, if you are self-taught, you should also utilize feedback as well. Always re-examine your learning process to get better. Feedback also enables you to switch learning styles midway through your lessons.
For example, through this book, you are going to unearth the various ways through which you can learn anything faster. Now when you start your learning process and utilize feedback, you will be able to tell if you need a mentor, need to concentrate more, etc.

But you wouldn't know what you need to do more unless you give yourself feedback after a specific learning point. As much as we want you to go faster, we also seek to inspire you. The essential learning question of all time is: "Am I making progress?"

You have done well with a swift ability to concentrate, maximize time all under high learning conditions. You will also agree that you have made significant strides in your accelerated learning journey.

There is an aspect of accelerated learning that is so vital but often not considered. Well, we will be taking you through that aspect next as it entails you relying on someone else to learn faster.

All scenarios used in this chapter were presented to bolster specific ideas and make the idea much more relatable to learners.

Chapter Four: The Importance Of Mentors

Have you heard the common saying, "No man is an island!?" Well, this statement has become a cliché, but it still holds a vital truth about life and learning.

For anyone to succeed, he/she needs others. Of course, there are times you will want to take the lone walk. But you will agree that collaborating with someone else does help you get a better perspective on things.

Honestly, within the context of accelerated learning, if you want to learn anything FASTER, get a mentor!

From the first chapter to the previous ones we focused on you, what you can do, you must do, and how you can get it done. But in this chapter, the focus is not solely on you.

You will discover the importance of collaboration and how you can improve your learning abilities through reliance on mentors. When you think about a mentor, what comes to mind?

There is a various representation of what a mentor means to people, but we will explain it in simple terms here:

A mentor guides a less experienced person to achieve success in a specific area of life. The process of mentorship entails building trust between the MENTOR and the MENTEE.

The mentor models positive behavioural traits that the mentee emulates to get the most out of the learning experience. A mentor is a person who is dependable, authentic, and sensitive towards the needs of the mentee.

A lot of highly successful individuals acknowledge the role of a mentor in their success stories. We were all novices to a specific area of learning at some point. But with the right kind of guidance, information, and connections, we can do the impossible knowing that we are not walking alone.

A mentor can help you unlock many mental doors you may think are permanently locked. If you are with the right person, you can truly gain a lot of insight into what you should be doing right as opposed to fighting with your ability.

So in this chapter, you will learn all about a mentoring relationship, how to seek out a mentor, qualities of a good mentor, and how a mentor can help you with accelerated learning.

What is a mentoring relationship?

Mentoring is a long-term process that entails the transmission of knowledge and the provision of support from one individual to another. A mentoring relationship happens between a person with more excellent knowledge, experience, and wisdom, and a person who is less experienced in that area.

The primary ingredients for a successful mentorship relationship are trust, mutual respect, the definition of boundaries, responsibilities, problem-solving techniques.

Mentoring is akin to a teaching relationship where age isn't a factor. What matters is the individual's expertise and ability to share information on his/her success in an area that will be beneficial to someone else.

A mentoring relationship can either be formal or informal.

A formal relationship occurs within a more academic setting where their academic supervisors assign students mentors. An informal mentoring relationship happens when the mentee (protégée) chooses his/her mentor.

In an informal mentoring relationship, two people meet and discover that they share a common goal. One person is highly successful than the other and will be instrumental in helping the less-successful individual attain significant attainments.

So what we are dealing with here is the informal type of mentoring where one person takes on the role of listening and giving advice. However, in recent times, it has been advised that mentees also seek ways to do something or add value to the relationship they have with their mentors.

So even though your mentor has the advantage, seek ways also to bring value to the table. It could be a minimal gesture, but it will surely mean a lot to the mentor.

Now you know what a mentorship relationship entails, the next question is, how do you seek out a mentor in your chosen field?

How to seek out a mentor in your chosen field

Profile the successful people in your field

The first step is for you to profile those who are very successful in that area you wish to learn. Now there will be a long list of people. Unless you want to engage in remote mentoring sessions, you will have to settle for a person within your environment.

You will be looking out for a relatable person, someone you like and can relate with on any level. It might take a while to get that one particular person who will be your mentor.

Now you mustn't rush the selection process. Else, you will settle for a mentor you don't like and cannot work with easily. Take your time, study the potential mentor's history and his/her success story before making a definite choice.

Reach out

When you have your choice of a potential mentor(s), you need to take the next step and reach out to the person. Now there are varying ways to reach out to someone you want to mentor you so you can learn faster.

You can send a brief email stating your admiration for the person's work ethic, accelerated approach to learning, and success story. Then end the email with a humble request for a mentorship program with the individual.

In the email, you can also express your interest in that area of learning. Also, state how passionate you are about learning but you realized the importance of having a mentor work closely with you.

The potential mentor might reply thanking you for your kind words and inviting you over to meet at the office or somewhere else. In other cases, the mentor may want to know you better before meeting physically. So kindly answer any question he/she might have about your interest in that particular field.

Aside from using an email, you can make an appointment (if the potential mentor has an office). But ensure you show up early for your appointment, so you give an excellent first impression.

Now some highly successful people may be tough to track. Some may not even respond to emails (not because they don't want to but because they are busy).
If you try correspondence and it doesn't work, try a face-to-face meeting where you can express your desires to the person. You can also attend events where you will most likely see the person (don't stalk). If you meet the potential mentor at an event, do not bring up the mentorship discussion immediately. Instead, request an appointment, and if he/she asks what you want to discuss, you can mention mentorship. Also, state that you have sent emails but didn't get a response.

You can employ any method in meeting with the potential mentor, but the critical point to note here is that you must take a step!

Be direct yet polite with your request

Now you've got his/her attention you need to express your desire to become a mentee. Choose your words carefully and be confident while speaking. The person you are talking to will not only be listening to your words but also watching your body mannerisms.

Make sure that when you ask, you place accelerated learning at the core of your request, stating how you desire to learn faster and achieve success in that area.

Avoid resorting to flattery with the potential mentor. Don't spend too much time talking because the person is busy (show respect for his/her time).

It is possible that after speaking the person declines your requests on specific personal grounds. If you get a rejected application, don't project your disappointment.

Say thank you and try again with another potential mentor if the individual agrees to your request. Show appreciation politely and listen carefully to what he/she will say.

Different things can happen when you meet the potential mentor for the first time, so prepare for any eventuality.

Show enthusiasm and dedication

The same way you have shown interest by reading this book to this point, show some excitement, with your mentor. You are pitching yourself to this person and trying to convince him/her to invest time and resources on you.

As such, you must show some excitement at the prospect of being mentored by this person. Also, show enthusiasm for accelerated learning, you can share a personal story detailing your struggle with success in that area. Explain your conviction that with accelerated learning through mentorship, you will able to do more.

You can also express your dedication by showing your potential mentor how far you've come on your own. Go for such meetings with proof of work, then express your optimism at how you can go with his or her guidance.

Listen, even when you become successful in your field with accelerated learning, you will not want to mentor a person who comes with nothing. So when you show up for a mentorship meeting, try as much as you can also to communicate your success thus far. So your mentor is motivated by your commitment as well.

The qualities of a good mentor

Next, we are going to unearth the qualities of a good mentor for two reasons.

1. *So you can assess who you are working with and be sure that you are with the right person.*

2. *So that when you also become successful with accelerated learning in your area of interest, you will know the good qualities you should imbibe to help someone else.*

Now the qualities below do not represent ALL the qualities a mentor should have (we cannot present all here). The virtues below are the most important virtues a mentor who is keen on helping someone on this accelerated learning path should embody.

Expertise in your learning area

The first sign you must look out for in a good mentor is his/her expertise in your area of learning. For example, if you want to be great at Tennis, who would you pick to mentor you? Serena Williams or a tennis coach in a school?

You cannot settle for a mentor who is average with that skill; you are trying to step out of the average zone! So when searching, go for people who are over-achievers, people who have surpassed the goals and are breaking new records.
Now that's the kind of mentor you require! You need to take on accelerated learning with someone who knows what he/she is doing. Of course, a bulk of the work still lies with you, but with such a useful guide by your side, you will surely make progress.

So expertise comes first even before likeness, it is possible to like a potential mentor who isn't excellent with the kind of work you desire. Go for knowledge, and you will be on your way to phenomenal success.

He/she is committed to helping you succeed

A good mentor takes your success seriously; as such, you leave every mentoring session better than you came. One of the reasons mentoring is crucial for accelerated learning is the fact that you can keep track of your progress.

You will look back at where you were before mentoring and see that you've made a lot of progress. By interacting, listening, and executing everything this successful person shares with you, there is hope for your goals.

So you will know you've got a good mentor when he/she shows absolute commitment to your success in varying ways. An excellent mentor views your success as his/her own so they become increasingly passionate about ways they can add value to your learning experience.

Of course, you can tell when someone wants to see you succeed; it goes beyond what they say; it is all about what they do!

Always willing to pass on knowledge

Why else will you be with a mentor who is unwilling to pass on knowledge gained? Mentorship is primarily about sharing, so you must ensure that you are with a person who is passionate about sharing.

By sharing, we are referring to books, ideas, materials, and everything else that was useful to the mentor in attaining success and will be helpful to you as well.

If you and your mentor do not get to spend time together at every meeting, it won't change the level of commitment. You will know he/she is interested in your success by the level of openness displayed between the two of you.

Good mentors will always try to share knowledge with you at every aspect of your learning program. This willingness to share is because they know that the success of one point will lead to the success of other parts of your lessons.

However, do not become complacent with shared information. A lot of people make the mentoring process quite hectic when they underappreciate shared information.

Some people do not use such information, do not give feedback, or even acknowledge the positive influence the materials have over their lives. So the mentor keeps giving and getting nothing in return that shows the usefulness of knowledge shared.

You've got to encourage your mentor too by being proactive with useful, shared information. When your mentor sees that you are using what you get, he/she will be inspired to provide you with more.

The person is a good listener

Good mentors are great listeners to their mentees. You will surely have a lot of questions to ask and have a lot to say; you need someone who will listen and help you through this learning phase.

So if you observe that your mentor listens to you, then you've got a great mentor working with you. Listening is so crucial because it is the only way you ensure active communication, which is the purpose of the mentorship program in the first place.

Good mentors also refer to the things you say afterward. So maybe you asked a question about how to get a task done a week ago, and your mentor gave you an answer.

If the mentor asks you about your progress with the task the following week, then it means he/she paid attention to what you mentioned earlier. It is the little things such as listening that makes the mentorship process an enlightening one.

A trustworthy person

Above all, your mentor should be an honest and honourable person. Someone who can shield you from public criticism by being discreet with the work you both do together.

A good mentor is honourable, he/she doesn't go back on his/her words, and no matter how tough the journey becomes. Mentors will stand by you and their other mentees until they can replicate the success with you all.

An honourable person wouldn't divulge personal information of his/her other mentees to you. A distinguished mentor wouldn't tell you what he/she cannot do to impress you.

A trustworthy mentor will lead you through a learning curve that is meant to toughen you up and not embarrass you. Reliable mentors are truthful about their learning processes.

When seeking out for a mentor lookout for these signs in the person, they are very crucial. Ask questions about the person and seek answers from those who know him/her.

In some cases, you may have already started the mentorship process when you realize that the mentor is not an honourable person. Neither is him/her trustworthy. So what can you do? Do not continue with the process!

Listen, you are not learning all of these because you have spare time on your schedule, and this is a feel-good book. You have a purpose, so when the person who is supposed to help in fulfilling that purpose doesn't fit the bill anymore, walk away.

You cannot afford the luxury of wasting time with a mentor who isn't the right fit for you. Remember that it is a relationship; both parties agree to give their best. If you are not getting the best, then there's no point in sticking around.

Politely request for termination of the program while thanking the mentor for his/her time

How can a mentor help you learn faster?

The question above is probably the most important one to ask at this point. You are focused on accelerated learning, so why would you need a mentor? With the tips below, you would get answers.

Your mentor's accomplishments inspire you

When you get an idea of how you want to learn and the particular skill you are interested in, it might be quite overwhelming. Mainly because you will be setting a new record (due to accelerated learning).

Well, with a mentor who has accomplished a similar goal, you will be inspired to go right ahead and smash the goals. For example, the only reason someone will think about having more Tennis Grand Slam titles is that there are professional players who have gotten above 20.

Once a dream, desire or goal becomes relatable, you start to feel motivated from the inside thinking, "If this person could do it, then so can I." Your mentor will also share his/her peculiar challenges through the learning process, thus preparing you for the journey ahead.

So many people who try out accelerated learning give up too soon. They give up because of the absence of a mentor, they start to feel like a dream is too grand, and without self-motivation, they give up!

But here is an interesting fact, you can be self-motivated and still need a mentor because that successful individual becomes a walking and living version of your speedy goals.

You can avoid common pitfalls

When we reflect on our younger years and make statements like "If someone had told me this when I was 18, I would have done better".

Unfortunately, we cannot go back to the younger years to make corrections. What we can do is strengthen our minds now to keep up with life's journey.

But there is a ray of light within this discourse regarding how we learn, and the help mentors render us. Since your mentor has gone through the same process, he/she is the best person to help you avoid the curveballs

Think of a mentor as a map, an active one that prevents you from making the wrong turn. Only this time, he/she will assess your work based on all necessary parameters and give a verdict that will inspire you to go harder.

There will be times when you feel like you are doing everything right, yet you are not getting the results you seek. Don't waste further time trying to know what could be wrong, go to your mentor, and in an instant, you will get answers.

Connecting you with opportunities

When you start on a new path, you are relatively unknown within the industry. Even when you make significant progress with your practice, you will need help penetrating the inner circles of professionals in that field.

Well, you can't show up for an event you weren't invited for so who else can make it happen? A mentor! Another key advantage of working closely with a mentor is the fact that he/she has an established reputation in the sector due to the high level of success.

As such, when you work closely with such a person, he/she will take you along by ensuring your networking attempts are with the right kind of people. Gradually you will begin to build your network of highly successful people too as you grow in the industry.

A mentor gives you access to all of his/her resources. In most cases, this also includes access to a network of professionals.

Encouragement and support

We all need assistance and help as we learn because, at some point, you will feel overwhelmed. The concepts you need to learn in addition to other things you've gleaned from this book might feel a bit excessive.

A mentor is the best person who can encourage and support you because there is a higher possibility that he/she also had the same experience previously.

So when faced with a dire challenge or it seems like you can no longer handle it, speak with your mentor. You will surely feel better knowing that your mentor went through the same phase, conquered it and became the better for it.

Sometimes, while on this accelerated learning program, it may seem like you are going too fast, but in reality, you are doing just fine. So you will need someone to encourage and uplift you while cheering you.

Your mentor understands what it means to walk this path and take on this learning approach. He/she can keep you refocused when you are dealing with powerful emotions.

A lot of times, when accelerated learning is in focus, people don't talk about the internal struggles they handle. Not discussing struggling points is peculiar to every other learning process.

Instead, we focus solely on the results we want to get. Depending on what you learn; there will be times when it seems like you are alone (this is a feeling most highly successful people experience).

Don't give in to that feeling; the best way to not give in is leaning on a support system, which is your mentor. You will discover that you can overcome such challenges faster with a mentor than when you didn't have one (hence maximizing time and staying focused).

Learning progression

When you work alone, you can achieve a lot, but when you work with a mentor, you go beyond achievements to building a consistent pattern of success referred to as "Learning progression."

Your mentor shapes you into a person who doesn't see an end to dominating that skill area or field of learning. When you learn alone, all you think about is how to achieve but after doing that, what next?

Have you ever thought about what you will do next after you smash those speedy goals? But with a mentor, you do not only get access to answers on what to do; you also become aware of how far you can go with what you've learned.

Through your mentor's success, you see first-hand a person's long-term success rates with this skill you are learning. So it puts a lot of things into perspective for you.

As you relate with your mentor, you will know the next steps to take and the kind of measures to avoid. You will also know how to be bettered positioned for the future because that is what learning progression entails.

Learning progression also means that mentorship inspires you to reach out to others who may be struggling with learning what you've mastered. You can use your learning story to encourage them, and by doing this, by teaching others, you will also be learning.

There is every possibility that your mentor hasn't stopped learning; successful people do not stop learning. As such, you will be getting tips on how to take on advanced accelerated learning techniques.

If you were working solo, you would know all of these or have insight into this kind of information. Mentorship is empowering!

It is phenomenal what we can achieve when we stop looking solely within ourselves and seek help from those who have gone ahead of us walking in similar pathways.

From learning how to build concentration to the importance of relying on mentors, you have gained a whole lot thus far on this accelerated learning journey.

We are matching forward now with increasing success as we build on all of this practical information with a section on the distinctive role your habits play in the learning game.

Chapter Five: The Connection Between Your Habits And Learning Process

You are going to learn from someone very successful and exciting in this chapter, so do look out for him/her!

We all have habits, those rituals and behaviours we involuntarily perform because they are a part of us. Habits form gradually: from observing other people, from doing something repeatedly, etc. The point is we subconsciously imbibe habits, and they become a massive part of our lives such that they even affect our learning process.

If you recall your high school or university days, you must remember that one person who had a weird reading habit. The person may say he/she only read when it's a few days to the final examinations.

Well, as you already know, he/she probably always failed or didn't perform as high as those who started preparing early enough. Now that is an excellent example of how habits can affect your learning process.

You may not realize that you've got a bad habit.

It will only surface when you start to see the adverse effects on your life. This effect will be mainly on your learning process. So in this chapter, you are going to discover how you can develop good learning habits that will make accelerated learning easier for you in the long term.

But before we get to the main aspects of the book, you should know that habits are fluid. So whatever habits you may have formed in the past that have hindered your learning process can be modified to suit your current learning expectations.

It is also crucial to point out that Elon Musk inspires this chapter. Regardless of what you think about him, you will agree that he is a productive human being who thrives on getting things done at a rapid rate.

So before writing this chapter, we took some time off to study Elon, and we discovered some significant habits he possesses that anyone can imbibe to learn faster. As you read through the chapter, you will find specific quotes from Elon himself on certain steps you should take.

This addition means that the chapter is a combination of the steps you should take to develop new habits and the ideas gleaned from studying Elon Musk. It promises to be an exciting one, so let's begin!

Steps on how to develop productive habits for accelerated learning

Identify unproductive habits

The first step is for you to identify the unproductive patterns you exhibit intending to get rid of them. You may ask, "How do I know my unproductive habits?"

Well, you will have to become self-aware to discover the answer by taking note of the things you do. Take note of the things that do not add any value to your learning experience. Things you cannot help but continue doing even when they are not suitable for you.

For example, if you find that while learning something new, you involuntarily check social media. This habit of checking your feeds on social media so you can tell what's going on leads to lost learning time.

Elon Musk works for long hours being focused on a task until he achieves a significant milestone. Now he didn't become a very focused person just by doing it when it suited him.

It took years for him to develop that habit, the same way it will take you years to do the same. But you've got to start now!

You need to take this seriously because habits can slip by us without us knowing that we do them. It's like a child who picks her nose when she's nervous; she wouldn't say she does it until someone points it out and tries to correct her.

So many people have varying habits they do without being aware they are doing it. This unawareness is because they have done it for so long now that it has become like a second skin to them.

It will take a watchful eye and extra attention to detail before you can tell that you've got an unproductive habit. But as mentioned earlier, patterns are fluid, and it is never too late to change the ones you don't like.

The next time you set time aside to learn something, set a time frame for the activity. Now if you do not meet the time you set, you go back in your mind to analyse your learning situation.

Remember, we discussed the concept of self-reflection in a previous chapter. Well now is the time to use that skill, but this time, you will be reflecting on the way you handled the task previously.

Be like an examiner at this point and critically assess your response to the task. Where there unusual pauses? Why didn't you beat your deadline? What did you do to distract yourself?

At first, when you do this, you may not have answers, but you've got to keep on reflecting and then gradually you will start to spot those traits and habits holding you down. Immediately you place them, start getting rid of them by replacing those habits with something positive.

So back to the example that entails always checking Instagram while trying to learn something fast.

You can replace that habit with reading a blog post that relates to the skill you are learning.

By doing this when you take your eyes off the task, it will still be on the job, but this time in another way.

Build organizational skills

Elon Musk was once asked this question, "What daily habits do you believe has the largest positive impact on your life?"

His response: Showering!

Now, this response may seem like a joke or a playful answer, but there might be some truth to it. I have noticed that most people succeed with accelerated learning when organized with everything they do to aim at learning something faster.

Showering might seem like a too-easy response but think about it, don't you think you perform tasks diligently when you are clean, dressed and refreshed?

Being clean is an effortless habit, but most people do not take it seriously because of its simplicity. If you have not been an organized person before, maybe that is the reason for your struggles.

An organized person feels prepared to do what is necessary for that day. Why else do you get out of bed and quickly run to the shower to have your bath before going to work?

The reason we all have the generalized habit of taking a shower before heading out is probably that subconsciously we all agree that we achieve more when we do.

Developing organizational habits should start with smaller things like Elon rightly said: "Showering." Always ensure that your body is well taken care of and you are in a neat space all the time.

Be neat always, even if you are working at home where no one else can see you. Develop organizational habits because it will affect your learning process eventually.

Keep a tidy office if you have one, don't throw things on the floor because you can, use the trash! When you become organized, you will find that thinking at a fast rate happens naturally.

Let's use more relatable examples now, shall we? Have you ever been to a library? Regardless of the kind of library (public or private), one dominant trait is familiar with all of them: orderliness!

Libraries are designed to be organized and orderly because it is a learning environment. If you ever went to an unorganized library, then you probably went to the wrong place.

The reason most people insist on reading in the library is that they tend to achieve more with their books there. So think about your learning space like you would a library.

But for you to make the "Library goal" with your learning process, you must start practicing it. Insist on being organized before you begin any learning process.

Start with your hygiene, shower daily, change your clothes often, and generally stay personally organized.

Self-discipline and will power

Another habit you need to imbibe is that of self-discipline and will power which can happen when you take them seriously.

Sometimes to learn something faster, you need to cultivate habits that will compel you to commit to the goal.

Now there are two strings to this step!

Self-discipline leads to willpower, but the first part must be fulfilled for the second one to pull through. Not being disciplined makes you have a lack of willpower, also known as "Staying power."

It is excellent that you want to learn using accelerated learning techniques. But after learning, how do you remain relevant in that industry just like Elon is in the tech industry?

First, you need disciplined habits. These are habits that enable you to finish what you start regardless of the obstacles. The people who give up quickly sometimes do not want to do that; they find themselves doing it because it's a habit.

For such persons, it is easier to give up because it is something they have done all through their lives. As far back as their childhood days, they 'didn't see the need to do anything extra because no one was there to give them that push.

Well if you had that kind of childhood, I sympathize with you, but you are an adult now who is responsible for his/her traits. What are you going to do now? Are you going to continue blaming your upbringing? Parents? Guardians?

Come on; it is time to take responsibility for your life! Reform your habits by intentionally being disciplined. For example, if you knew that you needed to do 10 minutes of meditation to get your mind ready for a task, 'don't cut it short to 8 or 9 minutes.

If you consistently cut it short, when you are set to do the work itself instead of putting in the recommended 4 hours, you will put in 2 hours, and that is how the pattern continues.

The example above is how people develop unproductive habits. They think 'it's a few minutes and seconds; hence, nothing will happen (it 'doesn't mean anything).

But if you calculate the 2 hours of work you skip daily multiplied by the seven days in a week (if you work on weekends), then you will realize that those "Little" hours are not so little after all.

Self-disciplined habits will lead to willpower, which is the trait Elon Musk has that has put him on top and above of his peers.

Willpower is your ability to stick with that skill until you get what you want; it is a trait that Elon Musk portrays most decisively. His company, Tesla, 'wouldn't have made any headway in the world without it.

Willpower can be built up through habits that give you the strength to remain focused on what you need to get done. So when you get it right with self-discipline, willpower will become the next trait you will imbibe.

Deliberately chose to set a good example

Now you are wondering, "I should set a good example for who? Well, you may not know this, but people are watching you as you take on this new adventure. They are waiting to see how you move forward with your dream, and you have a responsibility to inspire them.

Elon Musk is an inspiration to all of us at the moment! He is the representation of what we all think we should be, and without him telling us to look up to him, we do because we all are attracted to success.

Musk is a demanding CEO, he expects so much from his employees, and this is also because he shows them that he is putting in the same level of work and commitment.

Elon Musk once told an employee that he wanted the employee to think fast and ahead until his head hurts.

Elon reiterated that he wanted the employee's head to hurt every night when he goes to bed as a result of thinking.

Yes, the above statement may sound very "Uncaring," but you should know that a lot of his current and former employees have a lot of respect for him because they believe that he brings out the best in them.

His employees were always able to do things they thought they were incapable of doing before Musk challenged them. Now I know you are learning how to use Accelerate learning techniques for yourself, but what is the use of knowledge if it cannot be shared or used to impact someone else?

Sooner than later you will want to reach out to someone else and if you don't build the habits that encourage you to set good examples, you will be unable to do this.

Always work on your tasks and lessons as though the whole world was watching you! When you develop this mind-set, it will cause you to become mindful of your work ethic and commitment to your learning process.

Musk puts in around 85-100 hours per week and works every day of the week. So when his employees think they are working too hard, he shows them that he is working even harder.

Create the habit of visibility with your work such that people see the effort you put in to get the kind of results you derive. The acclaimed best footballer in the world Christiano Ronaldo is always the first player in his team to show up for training on the field.

Christiano is also is the last player to leave the field as he continues to train even when the other players go home. He works on his skills in the football field and showcases the efforts he puts in so when he scores lots of goals and shoes brilliance with his powers; people attribute it all to his habit of working extra harder than everyone else.

Be visible with your work as it will also encourage you to sustain willpower. Elon's office is on the floor of one of his Tesla factories where everyone can see him work.

According to one of 'Tesla's board members, Musk works in the most visible place because he wants people to see him and find him quickly. When you deliberately chose to set an excellent example for others, you will be motivated to improve consistently.

So when you get involved with a group project or you become the manager over other people you can be an excellent example for them while motivating them to be cohesive and effective.

Habits that stretch your goals

One of the significant traits Elon exhibits is persistence with reaching goals even when everyone else thinks that the initial set goals are beyond innovative techniques.

Elon Musk has built this habit for such a long time now that the world has become accustomed to his ground-breaking product releases. When you start out learning with a goal in mind, train yourself always to see areas through which you can stretch those goals to achieve faster and more encouraging results.
Sometimes when you stretch your goals, it may seem like you are unrealistic, but if you do it consistently, you will not only make it a habit you will smash those stretched goals.

Stretched goals are goals you set beyond your current perception of your capabilities. For example, if you joined a fitness centre because you wanted to burn fat faster, you will need to put in the work.

However, when you show up for exercises, you will be willing to do ten push-ups because that is what you believe is fast enough. Then your trainer tells you, you've got to do 20 and you think that is absurd.

But because your trainer 'isn't joking, you get to work. You get to ten, feel tired, and then you have to press on because your trainer is monitoring you. Then you hit 20! You are incredibly proud and full of excitement at your accomplishments.

Guess what? When you show up at the gym the next day, you will be willing to do 25, do you know why? Because your trainer stretched your previous goals and now you are inspired to do more.

If you make this a habit with everything you learn, you will be just like Elon Musk, a man who has redefined the concept of success within the tech industry.

Most of the time, all you need is a stretched goal to push you beyond the mental boundaries 'you've set in your head. Develop the guts to go for things and levels you do not currently think you can achieve.

As you pursue these more important goals, you will be strengthening your mental and physical capabilities while testing your limits. Listen, even if you don't attain success with the goals sat first try you can still learn from the process just like Elon Musk does with is a company. Don't develop habits that help you do what you've done before or the level 'you've conquered previously. Your habits should be traits you exhibit now that are futuristic.

A lot of the disruptive ideas Elon Musk has experimented with are thoughts people assumed was meant for the future but alas! He takes decisive steps today!

Go for a full depth of knowledge (Be a T-shaped person)

So in life, there are two kinds of people:

The "T" shaped individuals

The "I" formed Individuals

The "I" developed individuals are those who are knowledgeable in only one area of expertise. They set out to learn only one thing and stick to it the problem with these kinds of people is the fact that they will have to rely on what experts in another area say a word for word because they only know one area.

Now with regards to accelerated learning, such persons will find it challenging to make switches with their chosen fields because they have a narrowed perspective that is inspired by the habits of an "I-Shaped" person.

The T-shaped individual, on the other hand, has an "I" (if you look at the letter T you will see the I) the "I" stands for being skilled in a particular area but also getting to know details about other aspects that contribute to the success of their chosen field.

Elon Musk is a T-Shaped individual who is known for operating in the tech industry but also has knowledge of cars, engines, space, planets, etc. Now the reason Elon does this is so he can fully understand the process involved in creating anything in his factories.

So instead of merely being the boss who dishes out orders, Elon sits with his engineers, asks them specific questions about the engineering process. As he does this, he can learn faster and spring forth ideas because he is knowledgeable in every area of his business. If you want to be a fashion illustrator, for example, you want to learn how to design clothes and fashion concepts on paper faster, which is excellent.

But if you only focus on the aspect of drawing, you will be building g yourself up to be an I-shaped individual. To get the fashion concept right, you will have to ask a tailor or fabric experts, and all of these will cause you to waste time!

However, a T-shaped fashion illustrator will try to get bits of knowledge on how fabrics blend to create a fusion of colours. The T-shaped fashion illustrator will also get the basic idea of sewing; these are traits that can become your newfound habits.

Even though Elon is not an engineer, he knows bits of the engineering process. So when he creates, he doesn't have to always look for an engineer to explain certain concepts to him.

Now being a T-shaped individual doesn't mean you should completely abandon the core of your learning so that you can learn other things. What we are saying is to become aware of different learning variables that affect the main idea you are trying to learn.

Elon didn't deviate from tech into television; he is simply within his initial interest (the tech space). He is yet striving to know more in other areas that affect his creations.

Being a T-shaped person allows you to become more creative with your solutions while looking at things from a broader perspective. Instead of the narrowed view, the I-shaped individual learns through.

Build a growth mindset

Building a growth mindset is the final and most important lesson on accelerated learning from Elon Musk:

He says:

"It is essential to have a feedback loop. Where you're continually thinking about what you have done and how you might be doing it better."

Elon believes that the best piece of advice you can give yourself is to continually think about how you can be doing things better while questioning yourself. This trait can become habitual if you commit yourself to do it frequently.

When you start out learning a new skill or an idea, you might stick to a singular way of doing it because you are a beginner. But from Elon, we learn that instead of sticking to that single way of doing things, you should seek ways of improving on the method.

When you become desirous of improvements, you will find that there are even faster ways of getting things done than the level are operating in right now.

Why do you think Elon is so successful? Aside from the fact that he is innovative, he also ensures that he goes beyond the "Highest" levels of success (this is the level most people strive to get to).

Regardless of the level of success Elon Musk attains, he is never satisfied, and you should imbibe this as well. When you start to learn and succeed, don't let the level of success make you feel comfortable enough to settle for a peculiar level.

I am not talking about doing this one day and not doing it at all again. I am talking about making this a part of you by developing it as a habit. When the accolades come pouring down on you with so many applauding your success, remind yourself that you are only still at the surface.

Now you should be proud of your accomplishments as you attain them but build your mind up always to remember that things can be better. Everyone thinks Tesla is excellent, yet

Elon keeps on reinventing the wheel because he knows that for accelerated learning to be active, he has to push harder.

The only way you can consistently push harder is by developing the habit to seek more. As you advance, be conscious of this simple yet profound reality: Things can be better!

There is always a faster way to do the things you think you have done at their peak levels. This level of thinking is "THE GROWTH MINDSET."

When this mindset becomes the basis for your new developed and well-formed habit, you will be intentionally stepping into the world of limitless success.

In that world of success, people like Elon Musk are already leading the pack.

Thank you to Elon Musk for teaching us so much through words and actions. As they say,

"If you are going to be successful, be like those who are successful, monitor what they do, and take the kind of steps that they take."

Your habits are a vital part of your life's experience; they are the things you do even when you are not conscious of doing them. As such, when you make things right with your habits, your learning experience can be productive.

Remember to stay conscious of the things you do and how you do them. Become aware of the little moves you make because those are the manifestations that will lead to more significant accomplishments.

Have you ever heard of the term **"Speed-Reading**?" the next chapter is all about the connection between speed-reading and accelerated learning.

Chapter Six: Developing Speed Reading Skills

Reading is the best form of learning, and this also relates to accelerated learning. Whatever you want to learn, there must be something to read about it.

For you to be swift with the learning process, you must learn how to assimilate several phrases and sentences at once.

Firstly, reading is the processing of text to understand its intended meaning. Reading often goes beyond looking at words as you will need to understand the relationship between such words and their implications (sense).

Speed-reading is a technique used to improve your ability to read quickly. Regardless of the format of what is to be read (digital or physical copies) with speed reading, you can grasp information quickly, and that is the essence of the accelerated learning program.

While the average reader reads about 200-400 words per minute, speed readers claim to read up to 1,000 words per minute.

Although reading entails the use of your eyes, ears, mouth, and brain, speed reading requires you using all of these senses effectively but with more emphasis on your brainpower.

Brainpower is crucial because speed reading requires the highest form of concentration. You need full, focused, and sustained attention to make it happen. For you to speed read, you will need to see and understand the words on the page while thinking along with the author.

You try to detect meaning as you read as opposed to the usual way of reading, which allows you to recognize sense after a while.

This chapter aims at helping you develop speed reading skills because it is a crucial aspect of accelerated learning. Again if you want to learn anything you will have to read, it might not be a book, but it will surely be some material.

Now all the techniques you will find below have one thing in common: you will have to AVOID pronouncing the word and instead hear the word as you read.

The technique mentioned earlier is "Sub-vocalization," which is a process where you skim through the lines or a group of words as you understand more quickly than you can say them.

For you to stop sub-vocalization, you will need to concentrate on blocks of words instead of individual words. You can achieve this by relaxing your face and expanding your gaze on the page so you can stop seeing words in their single form. The more you practice, the more your eyes can skim faster across a page.

Speed reading can be fascinating, but it demands a lot of practice with the right techniques. You will gain access to the best speed reading techniques in this chapter and ways to get the best out of them.

Let the speed reading training commence right now!

Please note that unlike the other accelerated learning techniques you've read through, the steps below are to be in the order it is presented here.

You will only get the most of this learning process when you stick to the steps one after the other.

1. *Read the Cover Page and Table of Contents*

Reading the table of contents is the first step, and it sets the foundation for your speed reading abilities. When you get a material to read or a book, first read the cover page and then the table of content.

Why is this important? It is because it signals your brain and tells it the areas of the book to look out for as you read. A lot of people assume that speed reading is about learning fast so you can skip essential details, but this isn't true.

You need those essential details so you can grasp the significant subject matter of what you are reading. It is akin to when you are about to write a comprehension test, and you are told to read the questions first before reading the passage.

Now the reason for these instructions is because of the way the brain works. When you feed your mind with all of this prior information, you will be giving it clues and hints to look out for when you start reading.
Which only means that you will read faster!

2. *Time your reading*

After reading through the table of contents and cover page, you need to be conscious of how long you want to learn as against your previous reading timing. Do look out for the subsection that teaches you how to calculate your reading speed later in this chapter.

But when you have specific timing in mind, it will enable you to set a goal. Which means you wouldn't waste time being distracted either will you want to be a slow reader?

When you give your brain the task of having a specific timeline, you will be more committed to your reading process. Track your progress by checking the time as you read.

Always try to beat your previous ability as this will motivate you as well. You can also boost your timing by setting a reading goal which enables you to have a particular number of materials you want to read within a period and sticking to it.

3. Don't sub-vocalize

This step is also very crucial in speed reading! Subvocalizing means saying the words as you read. You must avoid reading to yourself because it drags you back when reading.

Some people even chew gum to prevent themselves from sub-vocalizing because they realized how important it is for them to put a stop to that style of reading if they want to read faster.

4. Read titles and subheadings

Within a book or text material, you will find several headings and subtitles. You must read these parts of the book because they provide insight into the content of the book.

This step is akin to reading the table of content and cover page of the book. So if you were reading material about how to cook spaghetti, you would find subheadings such as "Ingredients" and "Cooking methods," skipping through these headings will not enable you faster because then you will be trying to figure out the content of the section.

If you are reading a magazine, start with the title and keep it in mind as you read, so you always have the main idea of the write-up in mind while reading.

5. Use a pen or read with your fingers

This step is the most important aspect of speed reading!

"The Girl ate an avocado sandwich."

Some people will read the sentence above as:

The Girl, The Girl, ate. The girl ate an. The girl ate an avocado. The girl ate an avocado sandwich.

What this means is that they always go back to the beginning words in the sentence to try and pick the following words after it. This style of reading is known as visual regression because the reader isn't making progress with reading at all.

The time that person will spend going back to the initial "The" in our example, a speed reader will have moved on to farther parts of the text.so for you to avoid visual regression you need to use the most essential speed reading technique which is using a pen, your finger or a highlighter to read.

So the next time you read, place your finger on the lines and force them to move with you as you speed read. By doing this, you would understand the sample sentence just as it is:

The girl ate an avocado sandwich

When you get to "Avocado" and "Sand…" you can move on to the next sentence because you already know that the only thing a person can eat with an avocado that begins with the word "Sand" is a sandwich.

So you see that previous knowledge also aids speed reading.

When your eyes follow your fingers as you read through the page, you will find that your reading speed increases with time.

This idea is also the most critical speed reading technique because it prevents your eyes from bouncing all around the page. You are focused on one sentence ort part of the book at a time.

6. *See the groups of words*

As you work on avoiding visual regression, also read by focusing on a group of words. There are groups of words you must have read in the past that are familiar to you such that when you see a part of the group, you can instantly tell what the other part will be.

For example, if you are reading, and you see a word stating "The United States of America" you don't have to read through the entire phrase because the moment your eyes spotted "The United States" your brain already pre-informed that you know the word.

So you complete it and move on. When you train your brain to read through groups of words, you will find that you save a lot of time. You wouldn't be reading through numerous groups of words in the text.

If the material you are reading contains pictures and diagrams, you will need to focus on them as well. Charts, graphs, and other pictorial representations are vital for understanding and speed reading.

Why do writers include such pictures? They do, so readers can get the message they are trying to pass across in pictorial form. By looking at those images, you will get to the heart of the content without having to read every word or line.

Look out for the footnote below the diagrams as they will provide insight into what the picture is about as well.

While looking out groups of words, you can also highlight important words as you read. Now ensure that you brush your eyes rapidly across the entire page to get the "Gist" of the page.

Stop for a few seconds to highlight some words that will contribute to the overall meaning of the page. Start with repeated words; the severally repeated words may be the writer's attempt at putting that word in focus.

For example, throughout this section, the word "Speed reading" was repeated. This repetition means you can read it as a group of words, and wherever you see it, you will know that the writer is emphasizing the idea.

Search for proper nouns as there are crucial indicators, look out for italics, underlined words, and even words you do not recognize. All of these will help you get the most out of your reading experience as you will read faster and with understanding.

7. *Focus on the first and last sentences*

Another way to speed read is to read the first sentence of a paragraph and the last sentence of the section and merely taking a look at the middle. Now the fundamental idea of the book or material you will read is at the beginning sentence and the last.

When you try to read through every paragraph in detail, you will surely be lost. For example, with this book, in the previous chapter at the beginning, you were told that you would learn from "Someone" and then you were introduced to Elon Musk.

If you read that and the middle you will get all the ideas about habits and accelerated learning. While reading the first sentence, you will realize that it is easy for you to assimilate what is said because you have already read through the table of content previously, so you know what it is all about.

Reading these sections of the book also helps you avoid repeating and reading through words you have already read before as, in some editions, the original content may be the writer's attempt at reemphasizing some ideas and key points you may already know.

So most books already have introductions and summaries of each chapter try to focus on these. You can also read faster when you are familiar with the subject matter.

This step works better when you are reading familiar content, and you want to get additional new ideas.

1. *Go faster (yes, you can)*

You've got to go more quickly than you think is possible with speed reading. When you've utilized all the steps above, remember to push yourself harder because that is the only way through which you can truly harness this skill.

You can go faster with using your hands or a pen when reading to scan through the pages more quickly than you usually do, or you think is possible. It is always astonishing moment when you discover that by going faster, you are also able to retain and remember a lot of details about the content you are reading. Your reading speed can drastically increase when you become conscious of how fat you want to go.

A right way of enabling faster reading is to ascertain your previous reading rate before you started speed reading. This realization also means that even right now as you read this book, you should take into account your level of text.

So how can you calculate your reading speed?

In speed reading, calculating your speed is referred to as WORD PER MINUTE (WPM), and you can figure it with the steps below.

1. Read a portion of a book or material for 5 minutes at your average reading speed. Assume you don't know anything about speed reading at this point.

2. Take note of the spot where you stopped reading

3. Count the number of words in the first five lines of the portion you read.

4. Divide this by 5, and it will give you the number of words by lines (average amount).

5. Count the number of lines you read.

6. Now multiply the number of lines you understand by the familiar words on a string. (this would give you the number of words you read).

7. Divide the amount by 5, and you will get the number of words per minute.

With the steps above, you can calculate your reading speed and then after the calculation, make sure you set a new target for yourself because now you are going to read even faster.

The most beautiful thing about speed reading is the fact that it is a challenging way to learn. When you get it right with speed reading, you can also transfer the same skill into the other things you try to gain.

Remember the aim of speed reading is so you can apply what you read which means that even if you speed read 100 books if you don't take action by using what you learn from them, the effort will be in vain.

Do you have something you have to learn by reading? Practice now with speed reading and fall in love with the idea of going fast with words.

What do you remember from the previous week? Did anything stick in your memory?

Well, get ready to do better with your mind as we unearth the value of photographic memory.

Chapter Seven: Photographic Memory

We cannot round-off the process of accelerated learning without talking about the role of photographic memory. Photographic memory is also known as an eidetic memory that entails being able to recall names, images, numbers, words with a lot of precision.

To learn faster, you must be able to train your memory to be able to recall vital information that goes through your mind. The notion behind a "Photographic" memory is that it is like a photograph in your memory bank. You can retrieve images and content from your memory.

You can also view the photo whenever you want to, zoom in on it, and even share its content with someone else. A lot of us do have a photographic memory; we can visualize things we've seen before all over again.

But we need to heighten the ability by being conscious of it and developing it further. For instance, you may remember a particular street you've been to or a place you've previously visited when asked.

A photographic memory is an asset to anyone keen on accelerated learning. As you learn, you will have to recall a lot of previously taught lessons that will empower you to maintain consistency with your knowledge.

With a photographic memory, you can learn how to do something new by relying on previously learned information. As you learn, you also grasp details, concepts, steps, colours, and other aspects of learning faster.

Various parts of the brain mature at different times and the age of adolescence is a crucial stage of that change. From that age, we start to develop a sharp memory, but other factors also influence it.

Some of these factors include genetics, brain development, and personal experiences — the things you continuously do make a difference as well.

This book will help you identify your photographic abilities and harness it by showing you ways through which you develop it entirely.

Be more observant

The best way to build up photographic memory is by being vigilant. Don't merely look at things, see them for what they are, and take them into your mind. When eating lunch, avoid eating the salad alone, also look at the colours of the vegetables. Try to retain information as you can about the restaurant and the environment.

So when you do this, it sticks in your mind and when someone asks what you had for lunch two days later, you will have an answer. Even if you don't recall the exact name of the salad, you can say "Salad" because you were very observant during lunch.

Successful people sometimes rely on their photographic memory to replicate a pattern that worked for them in the past or with a previous deal. You will also be an asset to your company as an employee who has a photographic memory because everyone will rely on you for your unique accelerated techniques.

Take note of patterns

Another way you can give your photographic memory a boost is by studying patterns. Systems lead to complete structures, so if you know the trends of a particular skill or idea; you will be building photographic memories.

How do you prepare a classic Watermelon Cocktail? You get the watermelon and extract the juice, get the other ingredients (based on your preference), and you create your drink.

Now you wouldn't need to remember all the steps all the way. If you can stake note of the first patterns, you can execute that skill anywhere and in record time.

So the next time you want to create a watermelon cocktail, remember the watermelon, glass, and then every other step will come to your mind.
For some other tasks with more extended patterns, don't worry about what you can do. Break the method into groups, get a photographic image of them sand store them in your memory bank.

Practice remembrance daily

Through this book, we have reiterated the importance of practice because that is the core of accelerated learning. The more you practice you better you become. The same message on method applies to developed photographic memory through the act of remembrance.

As a child, if someone promised you a gift you remembered. You also ensured that the person fulfilled his/her promise else you would cry and throw tantrums.
Now, as an adult, you probably can't remember the essential things happening to you because you do not take proactive steps towards learning through remembrance.

If you were going to learn how to assemble a car in a factory, you would have to practice remembrance to do it faster than the expected time. Joining a car is like doing the same thing all over again with few alterations.

So if you can remember how to do it with one car, you will become an expert by the time you assemble the fourth car. Remembering works perfectly well with a photographic memory, and there is a way to ascertain this through something you do every day.

When you get into a cab to go home in the evening, and the driver takes a wrong turn, how do you know that the path is the wrong one to follow? It is because you have a photographic memory (subconsciously developed) on the route to your home.

Back to remembrance, try to practice it to become extremely good. Due to the importance of memory to our overall conversation, we will be taking you through effective strategies for remembering

1. Be interested in what you are learning

If you are not interested in what you learn, then you can forget about even remembering any of it. Whatever you learn should be of interest to you also if it is something you are compelled to learn.

Interest breeds higher levels of remembrance!

You will always easily remember what interests you. This fact is the reason why before you settle for a skill using accelerated learning, you should be sure that it is something you like.

2. Link what you learn with what you know

Whatever you are learning now is undoubtedly connected to something you've learned in the past. So by linking them, you will be creating a pattern in your mind.

This pattern enables you to remember one thing when the other idea comes to mind. For example, if you are currently learning how to play a musical instrument, and you used to play another organ in the past, link both playing experiences together.

So you need to remember how to play one of the instruments to recall how to play both. There is always a connection between everything we learn, find it, and use it to boost your level of remembrance for increased photographic memory.

3. Use bedtime

The night time before you sleep is also another opportunity for you to practice remembrance. But you must be intentionally consistent with this approach for you to see it work.

When you get set for bed, don't go right ahead and sleep. Try to recall everything you learned that day in detail. By doing this, you are creating a photograph of it mainly for your memory bank.

Sometimes even when you sleep, you will find that you dream about that activity you thought about because it is already in your memory. Let night and bedtimes be opportunities for solidifying your remembrance skills.

4. Remember little things; it will lead to bigger things

When trying to develop your remembrance skills, start with the more straightforward stuff before building up to the bigger things. To begin with, your clothes, food, friends, birthdays, anniversaries.

In the modern world, it is not easy for us to intentionally remember. But that is what accelerated learning is all about: helping you achieve what everyone else thinks is "Impossible" or too "Difficult."

Start today; remember your child's best friend's name. Remember what you ate in the morning, your boss's wedding environment and every other thing that matters around you.

By doing this consistently, you will also be able to remember those big things that cut across your work, skills, and lessons.

5. *Try to recall in a noisy environment*

Most people find it very easy to recall and remember anything so long as the environment is quiet enough. However, that is on the "Average" level. You need to go beyond that as it is easy to remember when all is quiet.

But if you need to recall a detail to achieve something faster and you are in a noisy environment, what are you going to do? More importantly, if you CAN remember anything you've learned in a noisy environment, then it means that the idea engraved in your mind is permanent.

So start practicing today by intentionally taking yourself away from your comfort zone. When you are out with friends at a party, check on your mind and the ideas you have learned.

The more you can remember what you have stored in the recesses of your mind in unconventional areas, the more you strengthen that memory.

Build a memory palace

Do you remember what you ate for lunch two days back or yesterday? Now you are combing through your mind trying to recall if you remember. It means you do have some photographic memory skills and if you don't, you are not alone.

Some people do not recall their home landline numbers as well without looking at their mobile phones. A lot of adults find it challenging to remember the birthday of more than three members of their families.

Numerous people cannot remember more important things than what they had for lunch. But you can correct this and do better with your memory skills by building a memory palace.

When you have a memory palace, you will find that you can easily recall the activities you engaged in previously, which also includes your learning experiences.

A memory palace makes everything more comfortable for you; it is like a hard drive in your mind you go to and download facts. So let's say you created an app for a company and now two other companies want you to do the same thing for them but within a shorter time frame.

Instead of feeling overwhelmed by the task, all you have to do is go back to your memory palace. Pull out the data you need from the information you've stored.

You will be able to complete both tasks in record time because you are not relying on manual guidance anymore. You are relying on the information you've stored on how you created the app previously.

In the olden days, how did the people navigate through cities and towns without signposts and Google maps? They used the same memory palace technique. So how can you build a memory palace?

First, you need to create a place in your mind that is safe for the accurate information you want to store. The palace could be your office in your consciousness or your home. But you need to think about the place in detail as this is where you build your memory palace.

Next, you construct the images which are the things you want to remember frequently. Go for things that stand out in line with what you do, bright colours, and specific objects.

In your mind, walk into your memory palace and place these items there. You need to actively do this by visualizing yourself, opening the door of your memory palace, and storing the information.

When you've done this, do something to distract yourself for a while. Now the reason you need a little distraction is to ascertain if the information stored in your memory palace is intact.

Go for a walk, listen to music, and then come back to your memory palace. Try to think about the information you stored, can you see it in your mind?
Can you see the stored photographic image?

If you can, then you have successfully created your memory palace. All you need to do now is continually update your memory palace with more information while expanding the reach of your photographic memory.
You can create several memory palaces in your mind with different content. Your brain can handle so much more than you think, so don't assume it will be too much.

Visualize your learning

As you learn the new skill using accelerated learning, try to visualize the entire process. For example, let's say you want to learn how to cook the most delicious spaghetti in your city.

Now you are with the recipe, as you study to try to visualize the entire process from the moment you start preparing the ingredients to when you cook. You must feed your brain with a lot of colours from the cooking process.

Think about the green bell peppers you are going to use — the length of the spaghetti, the colour of the sauce and even the sounds from the kitchen. When you get to the kitchen proper to start cooking, you will find that you can easily rely on the details you visualized previously.

Now, after cooking, you will shave stored all of the information of the entire proocess in your memory. The next time you want to prepare spaghetti, you wouldn't need to look at the recipe word for word anymore. You will have clear images in your memory on how to cook the dish.

By visualizing the learning process, you will be boosting the strength of your photographic memory, taking in details and become familiar with every aspect.

So when you are expected to perform the same task again at a faster rate, you would surpass the scheduled time of delivery because you've got a photographic memory.

A photographic memory also works well with even more technical skills when considering accelerated learning. This fact is because it enables you to replicate a process multiple times, and that's when people refer to you as an "Expert."

All you had to do was visualize the process in your head. Visualization happens by snapping photos with your eye and storing it in your brain. Have you ever listened to classical music or being at the opera?

If you had, you would be amazed at the ability of the orchestra to perform in the most organized way without having to read from any paper most times. What they did was to visualize the entire performance in their heads and build up photographic memory.

So when it is show time in several cities, they perform excellently well because of the power of visualization. The same principle applies to actors and actresses who become so good at playing a specific role that they earn an Oscar.

What did these actors do to make them stand out? They implemented the power of visualization through a photographic memory.

The next time you want to learn something g does not learn passively! Passive learning is when you read through the lesson or take action without paying attention and visualizing the process.

Retain as much detail about the skill and then the next time you have to do the same thing you will surely be amazed at your speed. Your mind will be easily accessible for you to pull out the photographic resources you require to go faster and better.

With a fully developed photographic memory and other skills, you have designed, you are ready for the last section of our journey. The next chapter focuses on self-development!

At this point, if you need to take a break from reading then you should take a break.

We are going into the final chapter, and it entails a lot of serious concepts that will finalize your accelerated learning program.

Chapter Eight: The Concept Of Self Improvement

Did you take a break before continuing with this chapter? Do you feel relaxed enough to round off the experience? If yes, you are on your way to becoming a knowledgeable individual who is aware of techniques and methods through which he/she can learn anything faster.

This chapter is the last in this book, and it entails the fundamental concept of self-improvement.

When we are focused on learning, it is easy for us to concentrate on the skill or job at hand solely. We become entirely oblivious to the fact that we need to practice self-development.

If you are only learning new things without building yourself up, you will find that you are proficient in that skill you are learning. But every other area of your life is not progressive.

Now we started by letting you know that with accelerated learning, you can learn anything at a faster pace. So we shared ideas on speed reading, relying on mentors, etc.

As we round off, you should know that while using all of these steps, methods, techniques, and ideas, you must be actively involved in the process of self-development.

You must be an all-round person who is not only knowledgeable in the area you want to learn new ideas but with life generally. When you are an adequately developed person, you will be able to integrate all the lessons you gain using accelerated learning entirely.

So while learning other ideas speedily, you are also adding value to your life. A valuable person will always want to do more, achieve more, and become more.

This chapter is all about value. The section presents to you those steps and ideas you can implement that will enable you to become a man or woman who is skilled in numerous areas of life. You will still have a firm grip on developmental skills.

Personal development is a lifelong process; you may decide to learn something using accelerated learning techniques for a week or a few months. But with personal growth, you are on it for the rest of your life.

You need to dedicate little portions of time to improving yourself daily. Then watch yourself grow into a brilliant, T-shaped person who is living life on his/her terms.

You were told to take a break initially because you will be discovering some new and exciting ideas on self-development. As such, you must be 100% attentive.

These ideas will perform dual functions:

1. *Consistently empower you to do more with accelerated learning*
2. *Help you live a truly fulfilling life*

After reading this book, you will be set to take on the next phase of your life with so much excitement because your knowledge base is complete.

Shall we begin?

Identify with a vision for your life

A life without foresight will be a complacent one. Foresight enables discipline; a disciplined person will always want to increase his/her value in life, which leads to self-development.

So it all begins with vision!

You need to find your vision in life, so it imposes the discipline for you to work hard towards achieving it. Perception is different from setting goals!

Vision is the entirety of your life's existence, it is the concept you live for, and you are in pursuit of every day. Your goals are the connecting bridges you use to attain your vision, but goals will be unimportant without vision.

Steve Jobs, before he died, had a vision for Apple. Even in his absence today, Apple still thrives because he laid the groundwork through persistent innovation and never-ending self-development efforts.

When you know your purpose, you will never waste another minute doing unproductive things. You will take the content of this book even seriously because you know you've got a short time to fulfil your vision.

We tend to admire people who have a vision for their lives because they are often the most self-developed individuals in the world. Why do you think we pay money to watch a tennis competition or a football match?

The athletes share their vision with us, and then we watch them take on numerous tasks to bring the concept to life. When they lose, we feel like we lost with them, and when they win, we celebrate like it is our win.

That's the power of vision!

Why did you decide to learn so much about accelerated learning? Why are you still reading this book? There is a reason why you may not know the defining idea now, but it's within you.

You've got to find your reason so you can also enjoy the same feeling of accomplishments like the athletes. A person of vision expects progress and works towards it consciously.

Such a person doesn't waste his/her time watching television or hang out with the wrong people. As a person of vision, your life becomes very "Tight" and narrow, you only give attention to what matters, and that is how you will fulfil your goals.

Vision also simplifies your life!

Bill Gates doesn't have to read books on how to care for a dog every day because he knows his vision in the computer world already. So he will narrow all of his energies into self-development patterns that will make him even more competent in that area.

Vision controls your choices!

Once you know what you want to be maybe a great tech investor, then you will see that you need to spend time at Silicon Valley. When you know what to do, you automatically know the roads you shouldn't be taking and the paths to take.

Vision defines what you will do in life!

With vision, you know your destination. You are on your way now to success, you also already know where you will be and the successes you will have in the future.

You were not born to do everything; in fact, you do not have a lot to do in life; you only need to do one thing! Look around you; look at the people you admire and respect the most. Even though they have diverse platforms, they are all still within that one thing they are meant to do.

When you succeed at that one thing, you can expand and start using the other talents you have. But first, you must identify your vision and purpose in life.

Even with accelerated learning, if you are not clear on what you want to achieve, you will stop midway a lot of times. You cannot go fast without vision!

The stress we complain about most of the time when learning and engaging in self-development happens when we don't know what to do (visionless). But when you meet a man or woman with the vision, you will find that he/she is not stressed. Yes, there will be challenges, but each trial will be surmountable.

How do I know the vision for my life?

Think about things that you believe when you do them will give you a feeling of satisfaction and fulfilment. Think about things that you would do courageously that will cause you to be satisfied with life.

Think about what you can do with so much enthusiasm and joy without getting paid for it. Within all of these things lies the vision for your life.
When you discover that there is more than one idea, start the process of self-development for the attainment of accelerated learning with the most profound insight.

This step is so exciting because self-development through the identification of vision is such a transformative process that will enable you to derive the benefits of accelerated learning speedily.

Be intentional about positivity

In every learning environment, there are crucial virtues you must imbibe, and positivity is one of such even as you seek self-development.

You've got to be intentional about the energy around you.

There are positive and negative energies, human beings emit these energies, and we derive them from our beliefs, perceptions, and experiences.

A person who has negative energy will never be optimistic about any learning process. He/she will always be a source of discouragement to people like you who are keen on getting better daily.

When you talk to such a person about self-improvement, you will be disappointed hence the reason you must ensure that you relate with people who exude positive energy.

Every learning process has its unique challenges, but that doesn't mean that we have to give up even before we start. Be a source of encouragement to yourself by showing up to do a task with a lot of positive energy, and you will be amazed at how far you go with the process.

Spread the same spirit of positivity to your friends, family, team members, and everyone else around you.

It is not possible to engage in self-development with a negative mind-set or being surrounded by negative individuals. You have come too far on this journey to let yourself down with negative energy.

Intentionally decide on the people you want to work with if you are to work with a group and they must be positively-inclined people just like you.

A commitment to learning

Every idea we've shared with you thus far has a core aspect to it, and the core of self-development is a commitment to learning consistently. There are various ways through which you can learn in the modern world. We will highlight some of these methods below but remember that it isn't enough for you to "Know" these, you've got to USE THEM!

Books

You are already reading a book right now, and I bet you have learned a whole lot from the first chapter until this point. So what are you going to do? Keep on reading!

Someone once said that the secrets we seek in life to better living are in books and it is true! If you are not reading books, then you are not getting a complete self-development experience.

Now the unique aspect about reading is the fact that you can read across all genres. There are books to read in every sector, idea, thing, etc.

While some books are inspirational, some others may be great for building up your vocabulary. This book taught you how to speed read already. So all you need to do now is get the most out of books by reading at all times.

Technology has also made reading easier through E-books, so now you've got access to a myriad of materials that inspire and uplift you daily!

Read because you are interested but also read because you are curious.

Read to discover new knowledge and learn to gain more!

Books will always take you further than you can imagine.

Podcasts

Podcasts are free, and we all have mobile phones, so nothing should stop you from adding value to your learning experiences through podcasts. There are varying topics you can gain insight on just by listening to podcasts. More often than not, you will be very impressed by the depth of knowledge you get from podcasts.

Download a preferred podcast app, search for topics that interest you or the issues that will fuel your curiosity. You can also search for professionals. Some experts have podcasts channels.

Utilize your time correctly by listening, learning, and developing yourself in a wide range of areas while on the go. Are you waiting at the airport to catch a flight? Listen to a podcast! Exercising on the treadmill, listen to a podcast!

You will become a reservoir of knowledge and a T-shaped individual who is focused on one area but is knowledgeable in several other aspects. Now that is a great way to practice self-improvement!

Social media

Yes, social media is the most viable platform for self-development at the moment now. Social media shouldn't only be a platform for you to post pictures, get likes, comments, and engagements.

The people who use social media for self-development save a lot of money on some other resources because they get amazing content for free. Do you recall when we taught you in a previous chapter to become strategic with everything?

Well, you've got to become strategic with social media too! Everything you want to learn and everything you need to get better with is on the various social media platforms.

Get on Facebook, search for communities and groups of people who are passionate about what you love, join the conversations, get tips, and build new relationships that inspire you.

On Twitter follow professionals, experts, and successful people who drop nuggets and tips that will make you better. You can even interact with these "Big" personalities by tweeting at them and interacting often.

Use other sites such as LinkedIn, Reddit, and Instagram to stay inspired. The kind of people you follow on social media is a testament to the presence or absence of your desire for self-improvement.

Seminars

Seminars are more streamlined towards a particular idea or topic, but one thing is sure you will meet a lot of experts. Workshops don't happen every day, so you need to be with the right circle of people or have access to information that notifies you of an upcoming seminar.

At seminars, you get to join other people who are also passionate about the subject matter and learn from seasoned experts. These professionals have spent years gaining mastery of the skill or idea you seek.

If you were interested in the gynaecological aspect of medicine, maybe you are a graduate from the university, and you want to stay updated with the current trends in the sector, then you must be ready to attend seminars.

Most seminars focus on contemporary issues with the conveners keen on providing solutions through thorough research papers from experts. If there is a professional within your community, you admire in the tech space, medicine field, etc. there is a possibility that he/she will attend the next seminar.

We spoke about reliance on mentors in chapter four well; you can meet with potential mentors at seminars as well. Also attending workshops are an excellent way to learn more about public speaking as you watch others speak.

If you want to be a speaker as well in the future, then you should attend seminars. You will be learning more about the sector and developing your speaking skills through observation.

Online Courses

Technology has made self-development even more comfortable with the emergence of online courses. Listen if you are still struggling with a skill or learning something new, then you might need an online course.

Online courses are akin to being in school but remotely. You can learn, unlearn, and relearn anything from the comfort of your home. You will utilize assignments, take attendance seriously, and give feedback after learning.

There are so many benefits and reasons why you should take an online course. The most important is that you learn on the go and from wherever you are at that moment.

Regardless of the topic, you have in mind there is an online course about it. Most interesting is that you can add the certifications you get from such classes to give your resume a boost.

Most of the world's best teachers and professionals now offer online courses. Take courses to broaden your horizons, take classes to learn new ideas in the industry.

The different reasons for courses are what self-development is about! Don't wait for a problem to solve before taking a class. If you are curious about how a system works and there is an online course for it, go ahead and register.

When you know a lot, it enables you to learn faster and more effectively.

Further education

In a quest for self-development, you might want to take steps towards getting a more proper formal training in a particular sector. The idea of additional formal education might not seem very glamorous, especially for older people.

But it is never too late to chase your dreams and go for what you want. In some cases, the knowledge you seek can only be in a proper educational institution.

If you want to be "Certified" in certain areas, you must enrol with institutions that give such certifications. Always aim for the peak of your sector or area of expertise.
The higher you aim, the more you might want to get additional knowledge. Hence, the reason top CEOs in the world still enrol at Harvard Business School to learn more.

Your speed with accelerated learning will also be on the increase because now you have access to well-researched educational materials tailored for a particular skill.

YouTube

Another precious learning resource you should use is YouTube! You can type anything into the search box and get a variety of answers from vloggers. YouTube has become increasingly popular in recent times because learners are becoming much more visual.

We love videos because we learn faster from them, and we can use all of our senses at the same time. You get to watch, listen, and even read in some cases.

With YouTube, complex ideas become simplified, lessons are relatable, and you can go back to a video multiple times for increased comprehension.

YouTube also encourages micro learning, which is the process of learning more significant concepts in bits and pieces until you become very knowledgeable in that area.

What you get with YouTube is a wealth of resources that will be useful to you in your quest for accelerated learning and self-development. You can start integrating YouTube into your learning experiences by searching for answers daily.

Travel
Traveling is a form of learning, and it is a process of also developing yourself. When you visit a different place, your mind becomes open to the limitless possibilities you have in the world.

We have talked about the importance of studying the lives of successful people if you want to be like them.

Well, a prominent trait of incredibly accomplished individuals is that they travel. They don't stay confined in one area, and this empowers them for global domination when creating solutions.
But more importantly, traveling enables you to learn new ideas and embrace new cultures.

If you can afford it, travel at least once in a year to someplace new. Be open to the lessons this new place will teach you, and when you come back, you will be amazed at the sudden changes you will make in your life for the better.

The fact that you are so keen on accelerated learning doesn't mean you shouldn't take time off to travel. When you travel, you learn, when you discover you grow, and that is when you can fully take on accelerated learning.

Eradicating procrastination

A good self-development advice you will receive is to avoid procrastination. Two kinds of people are reading this book right now:

1. Those who will immediately seek ways to implement the lessons even in the smallest ways possible.
2. Those who will set the task of implementation for another time.

So the people in the second group will say they will start using what they've learned next week or next month or some other time than now. What they don't realize is that no one has complete assurance of tomorrow.

Someone else in the first category will take action and always remain one step ahead of those in the second category. The people in the first group understand how time maximization worked (refer to the chapter on time for more insight)

The more you say "I will do it later," the more time you give yourself NOT to do it. No one sets out to procrastinate; it builds up gradually until it becomes a lifestyle.

Then you look back at your life and realize that you haven't done anything about your experience in terms of learning and growing. Self-development is something you must do daily even on days when it doesn't feel convenient.

By always putting the tasks and activities you should do for another time, you delay your levels of success. You also deprive yourself of several opportunities to learn and perfect your skills.

If you are on the first group of people who are doers, in addition to the commendation you got at the beginning of this section, you get praise for being a proactive person.

Now for those who never get to take action, it is not too late to begin. Today is a good day to take action (haven't we said this all over this book already?)

Then kick procrastination out for good! You have received the information you need to take on accelerated learning, and now we are giving you access to self-development plans.

Take advantage of everything you've received and added some value into your life by avoiding the practice of procrastination.

Do it afraid

When we introduced Elon Musk in a previous chapter, you may have felt impressed by his accomplishments and then reading about other people as well is inspiring.

But underneath that inspiration and motivation, you feel the fearful sensation. You deal with these issues internally as you ponder on your vision and wonder if you will ever make it or achieve your set goals.

I want you to know that fear is a common emotion successful people deal with even as they take the self-development path. Why do you think people are mediocre, not seeking to be self-developed? Their reason for mediocrity is because they are afraid.

Such persons hold themselves back all the time because of the fear of "What if it doesn't happen?", "What if the vision is bigger than my capacity?" so they stay by the side-lines, watching others succeed.

Your journey with this book is an indication that you are not for the side-lines. You are the world stage with success spotlights all around you!

First, you must become familiar with the emotion called fear by doing whatever you need to do afraid!

Take the next step, do the great things you need to do while being afraid, but regardless of the fear keep on moving! The most crucial thing to do is move forward.

A lot of times we allow fear becloud our sense of judgment, we feel overwhelmed by what we see in others and wonder "Can I do this?" s

Well here is the fact of the situation: fear will always be there within you, but you can thrive regardless of that emotion. Do you think that those who succeed exceedingly do not feel fear?

Most of the people you admire, lose money. They get into bad deals, make mistakes while learning, and even develop cold feet when they are set to launch something new.

But they go ahead despite their feeling because they understand a vital truth about accelerated learning and self-development;

Success is not about how you feel; it is about what you do!

So set that feeling aside, recognize it but use it as a motivational tool to forge ahead. Successful people do not rely on emotions to make progressive decisions because they realize that feelings are ever-changing.

Today you feel fearful, tomorrow you feel inspired, so if you rely on the unstable nature of your emotions, you will make mediocre decisions. We have talked about the concept of discipline repeatedly, so you don't need more discourses on that topic.

What you need to do is become PROACTIVE and less REACTIVE!

Reactive individuals feel the urge to react to every emotion; they are always on the other side of success. But proactive individuals are actionable people who have feelings but are not ruled by them.

Sometimes you don't feel like listening to that podcast or reading that impactful book. Other times you are too afraid to learn that new skill you need for the next level.

Such times exists, you must brace yourself for them and do what is required of you even if you do it afraid!

Health is wealth

Do you recall the last time you were sick? Seriously sick that you had to stay in the hospital? You will remember that in those times you didn't think about work, learning new things, the book you need to read or anything else.

All you wanted was to be well again!

No one achieves anything when he/she is unhealthy, which is why you need to be conscious of health when thinking about self-development. In a previous chapter, we mentioned the importance of taking a break when using accelerated learning. But now we are going beyond telling you to take a break. You must be conscious of your health status else you will lose everything.

The successful people you look up to spend a lot of time and money, ensuring that they are healthy because they are aware of the fact that if they break down, the vision breaks down.

Even when you have a structured team, your absence for too long because of illness, will affect your structures. So we are saying that self-development is closely related to the state of your health.

So as you push yourself hard daily to learn faster, remember to take care of your mind, body, and soul. Be intentional about your health by listening to what your body says. Your body is always speaking to you!

When you feel a headache, it means that you are dehydrated and your body lacks fluid. Your body feels like it doesn't have enough water, it signals the brain, and then you feel headaches.

Some persons feel headaches and ignore it. They continue working hard "Assuming" that it is "Just a headache." They take a pain killer and keep at it. When they stay at that rate, they will someday break down and find themselves in the hospital.

The doctor informs them that they are dehydrated. So they have lost time and energy when they could have adhered to what their bodies said initially.

This short but insightful illustration teaches on the importance of paying attention to your health. When you ignore the "Little things" like headaches, back pains, they build up to become big things like cancer and other terminal illnesses.

We want you to enjoy all that you have learned and the potential that comes with it but first take care of your health. Don't leave anything to chance; do not assume that you are in perfect health because you look healthy on the outside.

The person who can achieve a whole lot with accelerated learning is the fit one. Such a person is in control by knowing when to take a break and when to push harder.

Express gratitude and be happy!

When we become consumed with the idea of success, it is easy for us to keep striving and pushing for more without being grateful for what we have NOW!

This is probably not the first time you've heard about the importance of gratitude, but what have you done about the message? Now you are wondering what has appreciation got to do with my quest for accelerated learning?

Well, you should know that your emotional state largely determines your physical progress. The most profound emotional state that will affect the course of your life is gratitude.

I am most grateful for the access I have to knowledge in the area of accelerated learning. The more I expressed gratitude for this ability; the more propelled I felt to share my thoughts through this material.

After this book, I intend doing so much more with this ability, and it is all because of the role gratitude plays in keeping me motivated. I am sharing this personal experience with you because you must practice gratitude daily.

We can dedicate an entire chapter on the impact of gratitude in your life as a committed learner because it is so ESSENTIAL! How else are you going to do more in life when you are not grateful for how far you've come?

A grateful person has a high sense of worth, which makes him/her fearless in the pursuit of excellent results. Such a person can take on new ideas with accelerated learning. As he/she is continuously grateful for previous accomplishments, it becomes possible to do more repeatedly.

Through this book, we want you to succeed, but we do not wish to influence unhappy people. I like to believe that while reading this book, you were excited knowing that you have found answers.

But for some people the moment they are faced with a challenge while implementing what they've learned, they stop being happy. They also completely forget about the fantastic progress they've made (even the little steps).

You should enjoy success and its process!

We are all about empowering and inspiring you but think about it, what is the point in reaching out to people who are not happy with themselves? If someone gave you a manual on how to make ten billion dollars in a week, if you don't apply the ideas with joy, you will struggle.

Ultimately you wouldn't make money. You wouldn't learn anything, you will be frustrated with the process, and you will become a very disappointed and angry person.

Listen, whatever you want to do with accelerated learning should be done with a happy disposition. Happiness is an ingredient for self-development, and you can derive it easily by being grateful for your journey thus far.

Wake up in the morning, despite the events of the previous day with your learning process, say "Thank You." Do you remember the days you sought all of the knowledge you have now? You know so much now, so be grateful for the new experience.

If you think nothing elicits gratitude, look at your life, you are alive. So be thankful for that. Always express gratitude for the smallest things that happen to you.

If there is nothing else you can do daily, this one thing is sure; you can be grateful! Grateful people are excessively productive; they see opportunities where others see challenges.

Such persons are persistent, innovative, and daring. Practice being grateful, and you wouldn't need to search for motivation in others. Instead, you will be the motivating factor in people's lives!

Who are the people in your life?

We cannot isolate the idea of self-development from the people in our lives, they play a crucial role, and we will discuss this peculiar role now. Self-development is about the consistent action you take to make yourself better but have you ever heard the word "Influence?"

If you are fully present on social media, especially Instagram, you will know about the set of people known as "Influencers." These influencers have a large number of people following them, so they partner with brands and companies to promote their products and services, hoping that their followers will make purchases.
Now if there is an influencer you admire on social media, you will most likely be inclined to buy whatever he/she promotes. You will buy it because subconsciously that person influences you.

Now if someone you have never met, someone in another country, has such influence over you how about the physical people in your life? Regardless of your schedule or how enclosed you are as a person, there are people in your life. If you didn't pay attention to the influence they have over your life; it is time to take that seriously.

Again we look at the lives of people we admire, a lot of successful people have the right circle of friends. Most of them select their friends intentionally, and they are quick to let go of people who do not align with the vision for their lives.

This realization is the reason most people say, "It is lonely at the top." They need to continually let go of people who are not helping them achieve their goals.

We are rounding off with this chapter, but it shouldn't solely be the end of the reading process for you with this book. It should also be an opportunity for you to take a closer look at your relationships.

Are the people in your life inspiring and cheering you on to take on the accelerated learning approach you're invested so much time in learning a lot about using this book?

When building a self-development process, you must be conscious of those who are either cheering you on or pulling you down. There have been recent conversations about the role that energies play in helping us achieve success when considering our relationships with other people.

If you have built optimism through the years, be mindful of the company you keep. Don't surround yourself with those who are pessimistic about these detailed approaches. It's only a matter of time before you start believing them.

The voices of those around you become your inner voice!

What are you listening to/ who are telling your visions? Who are the people you call on when you hit a brick wall of challenges with your learning process?
Please realize that the process of self-development is one that is full of questions. As you ask you will get answers, and the answers will guide you into making the right decisions.

Never compromise your desire for self-development for a relationship with someone who isn't on your team, cheering you on and believing in you.

Bill Gates has always attributed most of his success with self-development and being successful in his inspiring marriage to Melinda Gates. Melinda Gates, in her recent book, also said the same thing about her husband, Bill.

So here you see two accomplished people who are helping each other remain at the top. It might not be your spouse or your romantic partner; it might just be your friend, sibling, colleague, etc.

The point is that you must have the right people around you to grow

Think of yourself as a plant:

Plants can grow anywhere so long they are planted in the right soil with the right conditions that include sunlight, water, and good soil. You are that plant that will become a huge tree, but first, you need the right conditions to grow (good and inspiring people).

Keep your eyes on the future

It is easy for us to learn what may be beneficial to us at this moment or in this day and time but while doping that we must always keep our eyes on the future.

This book will always be relevant to you years to come, but it wouldn't be the words that will matter at that time. You are already familiar with the words; what will matter is what you do with the words.

We all have a future that calls out to us; you have to listen and take steps that will help you go in its direction. Whatever you may be learning now might be a seed for future inventions. The only way to know is to keep your eyes on the future.

Highly successful people are continually thinking about the future. They do things today, inspired by the idea of what the future will be like for their generation.
So thought leaders and billionaires such as Elon Musk, Bill Gates, others continuously create products and solutions. They believe that these products will serve the present day and lay the groundwork for the future.
His idea is a pivotal one when considering the concept of self-development.

You can tell how your future will be just by looking at the decisions and the steps you are taking right now. Are you aware of what you should be doing?

So it takes us back to the first step on vision. When you have an idea of what you want to achieve, you will be inspired to work in line with that vision for the future.

Whatever you read now, whatever course you register for and whatever learning steps you take should be like a bridge. The bridge links your current situation with the future.

The idea of thinking ahead is the highest form of self-development you can practice!

Never forget this as we round off the journey!

The temptation to remain at a certain level through the years comes as a result of fear most times. We often feel "Today is enough," but then ideas are not static neither are they meant to stick to one person.

Someone probably thought about social media in the past even before the likes of Mark Zuckerberg but because he/she never looked into the future.
Maybe he/she even realized the importance of social media but didn't take strategic steps (no matter how little). Now Mark Zuckerberg's example is on a bigger scale.

There are other smaller ideas you could implement today that takes you closer to the future. Due to the in-depth nature of what the future would be, you will be compelled to read more than everyone else.

You will be inspired by the idea of the future to go one step ahead than everyone else because you carry the burden of the future in your mind. Let' use one last efficient example, shall we?

So do you recall when you were at university? You probably attended some graduation ceremonies, where you saw the best graduating students get their honours and commendation.

If you were a very deliberate student, you must have told yourself that when you graduate, you will also get top honours. So at that moment, you are present in your school, but your mind is programmed for future success.

Unlike the student who doesn't haven't such a resolution, you will increase your study times, visit the library more and take your assignment seriously. You will do other things at that moment that will help you achieve the goal when you graduate.

So when you graduate, you will walk on that stage with so much grace knowing that you deserve the commendation and you have worked hard for it.

Here is where it gets interesting, even if after all your efforts you do not get the top honours you have given yourself training in excellence that will be of immense value to you in other areas of your life.

You will never be mediocre again in your life after that training process. In everything you do, you will strive to be the best, and that is why it is a self-development process, it never ends!

Well, look who just rounded off an entire training program on accelerated learning! Well done to you! Life is about to be so much fun from this point, and you will be glad you had this experience.

Can you practice your speed reading ability now by reading through the concluding section? I think you should!

Conclusion

What a journey!

You have done well reading through from the beginning to this concluding section, and you deserve a commendation. Accelerated learning is a fascinating way of adding value to your learning process as you 'don't only get to learn fast; you also get to learn MORE!

We have gone beyond the basics of learning; with this book, you have genuinely gained access to the key that will help you unlock all of your learning potentials.

So here we are at the end of an incredible experience, the burning question is,

"'What's next?"

After reading an inspiring and astonishing book, what do you do next? Do you put it down? Tick the title off your reading list? Or do you take active steps towards implementing what you've discovered?

What you have in this book are words, but these words need to come alive through action. You cannot become successful with anything by only by reading; 'you've got to take action as well.

So it is significant that this book has inspired you but are you merely mentally encouraged or inspired to take action as well? The essence of going through this inspiring journey is to ascertain what you can gain from utilizing accelerated learning techniques.

What you can do is to decide on what you want to learn!

Think about all the past failures 'you've had at learning, and if you are up to it, take a step back to relearn them. Use the accelerated learning methods 'you've unearthed to go beyond the ordinary.

If you want to learn something entirely new then go right ahead, the point is that nothing can stop you now from doing what you want to do! You are empowered to take action, and the more you implement these ideas, the better it will be for you in the long-run.

Beyond the power of gaining knowledge is the power of execution!

A lot of people read, but few take action on what they learn — the reason there is a massive disparity between highly successful people and those who are not successful.

Genuinely successful people go all out to use what they learn because they recognize the importance of being proactive. When you are active, you become self-motivated to do the things you NEED to do instead of what you WANT to do.

There are numerous accelerated learning success stories; you are familiar with some of the names of people who have won in life with this idea. From Steve Jobs to Salvador Dali, Leonardo DaVinci and many more popular, successful figures you know.

So you would be joining this great league of men and women who refused to be mediocre by doing things the "Average" way. These people used accelerated learning in their time to achieve so much more, and you can do the same.

'That's the message of this section; YOU CAN DO THE SAME!

Listen, whenever you want to do something that will trigger a complete positive change in your life, you will face some stiff challenges. It is only natural for problems to surface because you will be changing the order of your activities and everything else that pertains to you.

You need to be encouraged, even in the face of such daunting obstacles. Stick to your vision and create what you want to see in the future today.

You can start using the program to add value to your learning experience as you discover more about life through new skills. The whole world is waiting to read about a new record set with a unique ability. When should you begin this process? What is the most suitable time to do it? 'It's now!

Best Wishes

Trustgenics

Limitless:

Master The Art Of Memory Improvement With Brain Training To Learn Faster, Remember More, Increase Productivity And

Improve Memory

Table Of Contents

Introduction

Chapter 1: Impress People with Expert Level Memory Recall

Chapter 2: Negative Effects on Your Brain Explained, Including Fatigue, Nutrition, and Hormones

Chapter 3: Apply Memorization Techniques to All Areas of Your Personal and Professional Life. Remember Names, Numbers, Lists, and Even Impress Your Friends

Chapter 4: By Memorizing a Pack of Playing Cards

Chapter 5: Discover the Secret of the Oldest Memory Trick that Dates Back to Around 500 B.C.

Chapter 6: Powerful Memory Techniques and Memory Skills to Increase Brain Function

Chapter 7: Protect Your Memory from Deteriorating Due to the Aging Process

Conclusion

Introduction

Surely, you have had instances when you forgot where you placed your keys, your doctor's appointment, important deadlines with clients, and even your wedding anniversary. You may have seen people and struggled to recall their names even though you remembered their faces.

Well, you are not alone. Millions of people all over the world experience the same thing. Just like you, they also blank out and forget stuff.

However, there really is no such thing as "bad memory". People forget things because they do not use their memories to the fullest extent.

Scientists have determined that the human brain is able to adapt and change in such a staggering manner – regardless of a person's age. This brain capability is better referred to as neuroplasticity. The human brain has the great ability to alter present connection, form new neural connections, and react and adapt in constantly changing means. All this can be achieved once the proper stimuli is applied.

Whether you are a student studying for the final exams, a working professional interested in sharpening your memory, or an elderly person looking to preserve and enhance the gray matter in your brain as you age, you can use a lot of strategies to improve your memory and mental performance.

A powerful memory can help you succeed in school, at work, and in life. It can help you learn faster as well as give you more opportunities to earn more money. Even if becoming a memory master is not your main goal, brain training will surely be beneficial for you.

So, if you want to improve your memory, start reading the following chapters.

Thanks for downloading this book. I hope you enjoy it!

Chapter 1: Impress People with Expert Level Memory Recall

Memrise founder and CEO Ed Cooke said that attending business school or getting a consultant is important in business. You can succeed on your own merits. In fact, Cooke spent most of his 20s joining and winning competitions. He used to memorize the order of sixteen decks of cards, for instance.

His experience is the perfect preparation for his role. After all, Memrise is an effective tool that helps individuals learn anything, from foreign languages to scientific facts. It involves the use of fun associations to make ideas or words stick. Later in this book, you will learn more about the strategies that they use to sharpen memory.

Likewise, Malcolm Gladwell brought up the theory of deliberate practice in his book entitled Outliers. This proves that excellence does not always have to come from talent, but rather devotion and hard work. If you spend thousands of hours on deliberate practice, you can develop a skill.

As the saying goes, "practice makes perfect". For example, typing may seem like a simple skill. You type words on your computer without even looking at your keyboard. You have already mastered the placement of the letters, numbers, and special characters.

However, you have not always been this good, right? When you first started to use a computer, you had a hard time typing because you did not know the placement of characters yet. As time goes by, you get better at typing. You get used to the activity because you keep doing it over and over.

So, what makes practice deliberate?

Well, there are certain characteristics that you have to watch for.

For starters, it has to require effort. Otherwise, everybody will do it and it will not separate average individuals from world class performers anymore.

It must be designed to enhance performance. It has to prompt you to push your limits and get out of your comfort zone. You have to do something that you do not understand and have never done before.

You have to repeat doing it until you nail it. Self-mastery is crucial. There should come a time when doing it becomes effortless, natural, and automatic because you are so used to doing it.

Moreover, it has to have feedback. You should be able to tell whether or not you are doing it correctly. This way, you can improve your ways in case it is necessary.

Daniel Coyle, author of The Talent Code, recommends choosing a target and reaching for it. Then, you should assess the gap between your reach and your target before going back to the first step.

Automatic Plateaus

Some people wonder why they need a form of practice that is different from a normal one. The answer to this is that performance plateaus are necessary for improvement and growth.

For example, a man may drive his whole life, but never develop the skills of a race car driver. After learning how to drive, his performance has plateaued and his skill level became stagnant.

In general, developing a skill requires full attention and effort. Eventually, the task or activity becomes automatic if you render enough hours in doing it. During this time, further improvement and performance plateaus should be aimed for.

Breaking Down Skills

In order for you to do an impossible task, you have to break it down into smaller possible tasks.

To deliberately practice, you have to break down one skill into smaller parts, each of which should be practiced. Repeat doing these parts until they become automatic. Then, you have to work on them further in order to attain refinement. Only then will you be able to say that you have mastered the skill.

For example, if you want to learn programming, you need to have certain sub-skills, such as familiarity with control structures and general computer literacy. You have to learn these basic skills before you can move on to intermediate ones, and consequently to advanced.

Before you can create an application, you have to be familiar with how stack works. You have to learn about the command line, as well as know how to use the Internet. Before you can be good at speed reading, you have to have a wide vocabulary. You have to understand what you are reading so that you can quickly move on to new chapters.

This is true for all skills, no matter how mundane they may seem. You have to master the most basic part before you can move to a higher level. Everything, from writing to solving math problems to playing a musical instrument, requires consistent practice.

Neutral Configuration and Paying Attention

Ralph Waldo Emerson once said that a man becomes whatever he always thinks about.

There is a connection between attention and neural reconfiguration. The theory behind it is that the brain wires anything that you focus on. When you lean on neural structure often, it grows further.

Consider mindless practicing, for example. When you sit down with an instrument or run through a song haphazardly, nothing sticks. On the other hand, if you focus as you play through a song, every note sticks. You remember everything. There is a scientific reason behind this.

Attention makes your brain grow. When you focus on something, it sticks with you for a long time.

How can your attention improve?

There are a variety of ways on how to improve attention, including stimulants such as nicotine, Adderall, and caffeine. You can also pay attention to attention, particularly by practicing Vipassana meditation.

You can also eliminate distraction. For example, you can turn off your phone or TV. If you tend to overthink or be anxious over certain things, you can set a specific time for it. Allot a worry period each day. This way, you can think about the things that bother you for a short while and spend the rest of your day doing important tasks.

Insight, Recognition, and Memory

World-class athletes and performers got to where they are today through consistent practice. They trained day and night, wasting no opportunity to improve their skill.

Anna-Maria Botsari simultaneously played 1102 chess matches in 2001 and won 1095 times. Marc Lang simultaneously played blindfold chess and won nineteen times.

You may think that memorizing board positions is easy for chess players and that it is in their nature. However, this is not the case. These individuals practiced for years. They developed their long-term working memory after many years of training.

The earliest proof for this can be found in de Groot's study of chess recall. He worked with skilled chess players and told them to recall various board positions. The participants did well when showed actual board positions. They did poorly when shown random board positions.

This study was then replicated a few more times in bridge, chess, dance, field hockey, figure skating, basketball, physics, computer programming, music, and electronics.

The theory behind this is that untrained individuals can hold around seven numbers in their short-term memory at once. Short-term memory is generally limited, but you may get around it through chunking.

For example, if you are given meaningful board positions, you may hold bigger chunks in your memory. When you read, you hold words in your memory instead of letters.

This is the way expert memory functions. Humans essentially have a glue function that occurs during practice. According to Herbert Simon, a chunk takes around thirty seconds of focused attention to materialize. A person of expert level has already created fifty thousand to nearly two million chunks. This is equivalent to four hours of practice each day for a decade.

Intuition

Intuition usually distinguishes experts. Take the blitz style in chess, for example. Generally, it works that every side is given five minutes on the clock as well as ten seconds for every turn. Based on the conditions, a person should rely on his intuition instead of thought.

It is not surprising that great chess players easily beat weak ones during blitz matches. Why does this happen? Where does intuition come from? The answer to this question is long-term memory.

You see, when your brain makes a chunk, it gets saved in the long-term memory. So, a chess master has already created thousands of chunks from his previous matches. He already knows which moves should be taken and which ones should not.

Intuition is when the brain recalls something it has already seen before and then matches the patterns that it sees in the present. So, when a chess player views the board, his long-term memory retrieves information that can be helpful. He remembers strong moves and similar positions. This allows him to take the right move.

Insight is the effortless and fast recall of cached experiences. Rather than compute something multiple times, you can simply retrieve it from your memory.

The human brain works the same way. When you encounter a problem or experience, you use effortful computation to deal with it. This is then chunked and saved in your long-term memory. When you encounter a similar problem in the future, you can use look ups to solve it.

The Mental Molasses Hypothesis

A single neuron can fire one to two hundred times per second. This is basically akin to a processor's clock speed in which every neuron is a processor. Brain neurons operate at a maximum speed of 200 hertz while a processor can reach speeds of 4 billion hertz or 4 gigahertz. This only shows that a central processing unit is actually twenty million times faster than a neuron.

So, where does the difference lie between the two? Well, a modern central processing unit may have four to eight processors, but the human brain has one hundred billion neurons. Hence, it can be regarded as a parallel processor.

Then again, the brain cannot compute answers to problems. It can only retrieve answers from memory. The human brain is a massive cache. It can compute, but it is slow. Thoughts are retrieved from long-term memory. Even in a conversation, you may notice that you are merely repeating things that you have heard or thought in the past.

In Conclusion

Humans are basically memory machines. Expertise is merely a result of how much chunks or specific knowledge has been stored in memory. Such chunks are made during deliberate practice, which requires intense focus. In turn, intense focus is required to produce neural reconfiguration.

So, how can you apply this to everyday life? You can use Anki to boost your chunk production. You can take a skill that you want to improve and break it down. Determine any weakness that you have and create an elaborate plan to improve the skill. See to it that you break this plan into smaller chunks so that you do not get intimidated or overwhelmed.

When you are done creating your plan, you should use the Pomodoro technique every day. Only focus on deliberate practice. Refrain from letting any distraction get the best of you. Refresh your mind and body through meditation and a good diet. See to it that you also review your plan and training periodically to ensure that everything is on point. Eliminate anything that does not work. Do not be afraid to get out of your comfort zone to try something new.

Chapter 2: Negative Effects on Your Brain Explained, Including Fatigue, Nutrition, and Hormones

Fatigue, poor nutrition, hormonal imbalances, and stress can all have negative effects on you. These factors can cloud your mind and cause you to perform poorly.

How Fatigue and Stress Negatively Affect the Brain

Fatigue can make it difficult for you to focus and manage your moods. It can even cause you to have mental block, irritability, and lack of motivation. When you are stressed out and fatigued, it can really be hard to do anything properly.

Stress, in particular, is bad for both the body and mind. It can cause unpleasant physical symptoms such as chest pain and headaches as well as mood issues such as sadness and anxiety. It can also cause behavioral problems such as overeating and anger outbursts.

Even worse, stress can have a serious impact on the brain. Whenever you are stressed, your brain experiences multiple reactions that are naturally designed to protect itself against possible threats. There are times when stress is necessary, such as when it helps you remember details. For the most part, however, stress is not good for you.

According to researchers, stress can shrink the brain's volume and contribute to mental health problems.

Chronic stress causes mental illness.

A study published in Molecular Psychiatry has shown that chronic stress can cause long-term brain changes, which in turn can make you prone to anxiety and mood disorders. Likewise, stress can cause mental and emotional disorders, including depression.

At the University of California in Berkeley, researchers conducted several experiments to look at the effects of chronic stress on the human brain. They have found that stress leads to the production of myelin-producing cells with abnormally low neuron count.

This occurs when the myelin in the brain becomes excessive and starts to interfere with the balance and timing of communication. The researchers also found that stress also negatively affects the hippocampus of the brain.

Stress changes the structure of the brain.

This is perhaps one of the most shocking effects of stress. Researchers have found that chronic stress can cause long-term changes in the function and structure of the brain.

As you know, your brain consists of gray matter and neurons. These support cells are responsible for problem-solving and decision-making. Your brain also has white matter, which consists of axons that are linked to the other areas of the brain. It is called white matter because of the myelin or the fatty, white sheath that surrounds the axons. These axons speed up electrical signals to allow information to be communicated to the brain.

When myelin is overproduced because of chronic stress, the structure of the brain can change and the gray and white matter can have an imbalance. According to researchers, those who suffer from post-traumatic stress disorder also tend to have gray and white matter imbalances as well as other brain abnormalities.

Daniela Kaufer, a researcher and psychologist, stated that stress does not always affect the neural networks and the brain in a similar manner. The positive type of stress can help people do well in the event of an emergency or challenge. Their brains can be wired positively, causing them to be more productive and resilient.

On the contrary, chronic stress only yields problems. So, stress either improves you or destroys you. It can either make you resilient or prone to mental illnesses, depending on the white matter pattern you have.

Stress causes brain cells to die.

Researchers at the Rosalind Franklin University of Medicine and Science have found that a socially-stress event can kill the new neurons inside the hippocampus of the brain.

The hippocampus is the area of your brain that is associated with learning, memory, and emotions. It is also where new brain cell formation or neurogenesis takes place.

The researchers used rats in their experiments. In one cage, they let two old rats mix with young rats for twenty minutes. The young rats experienced aggression from the older rats.

When the researchers examined the rats, they discovered that the young rats that experienced aggression had six times higher levels of cortisol than the ones that did not experience aggression.

Furthermore, even though both groups of young rats had the same amount of new neurons, the ones that experienced stress had a reduction of nerve cells. Thus, although stress may not affect the formation of new neurons, it can still affect their survival.

Stress causes the brain to shrink.

Anyone, regardless of health condition, can experience brain shrinkage if they are exposed to stress. In particular, the areas of their brain that is connected to memory, emotions, and metabolism will be affected.

According to researchers, the stress that you experience on a daily basis can accumulate over time and eventually result in mental illnesses. You may not notice the effects of chronic daily stress right away, but they can actually make your brain shrink when you get exposed to traumatic and intense stressors.

Researchers at Yale University conducted a study that involved one hundred healthy individuals. These participants gave information about the stressful encounters they have had in life.

The researchers found that being exposed to stress, no matter how much time has passed, caused the gray matter in the participants' prefrontal cortex to shrink. The prefrontal cortex is the area of your brain that is associated with emotions and self-control.

So, if you are constantly exposed to stressful situations, you can have a harder time dealing with stress in the future. This is especially true if you have to have integrated social processing, effortful control, or emotion regulation.

Stress negatively affects memory.

When you are stressed, you may have a difficult time remembering events and important details. Even mild stress can negatively affect your memory. For example, you may struggle to recall where you placed your car keys or your briefcase.

In 2012, researchers have found that chronic stress negatively affects spatial memory. This is your ability to remember details associated with location and spatial orientation. In 2014, another study has shown that high cortisol levels can cause short-term memory to decline.

In essence, stress can either help or hurt your memory. For instance, timing is among the variables that cause stress to affect memory. According to researchers, if stress is experienced immediately prior to learning, memory consolidation can be achieved and memory can be improved.

Then again, stress can also hamper memory retrieval. In their experiments, the researchers have found that being exposed to stress prior to a memory retention test can result in poor performance.

How Poor Nutrition Negatively Affects the Brain

For decades, experts have proven that the food you eat directly affects your behavior and cognitive performance. For example, coffee can stimulate your brain while sugar can make children hyperactive. Chocolate can also make you feel good.

In the recent years, however, further studies have been made on the nutritional effects of food on the brain. In particular, researchers have discovered that certain types of food affect mood disorders, disease states, aging, cognition, and brain development.

A major effect of nutrition on brain function is on cognition. Poor diet can negatively affect energy levels, mood, and sleeping patterns. Also, cognition can be indirectly affected by other brain function developments. For example, nutrition is necessary to develop sensory systems such as vision and hearing. If these systems are not fully developed, cognitive maturation cannot be achieved.

Nutrition also directly affects cognition during neurodevelopment and aging. Getting the right nutrients is absolutely crucial during these times. Otherwise, the functioning of the brain cannot be optimized.

How Diet Affects Brain Function

At the Neuroscience 2012, the annual meeting of members of the Society for Neuroscience, it was found that the brain's biological processes can affect serious medical conditions, such as obesity and diabetes.

The researchers used imaging technologies to study the way neurology affects dietary disorders. They found that what people eat affects what and how they think.

They found that the cognitive function of an individual is influenced by obesity. This means that more efforts are necessary to complete a complex decision-making activity.

When you skip breakfast, the part of your brain associated with pleasure gets turned on after seeing images of food that are high in calories. Also, skipping breakfast can cause you to eat more at lunch.

In one study, it was found that a high-sugar diet can affect the insulin receptors of the brain as well as undermine memory and spatial learning skills. Nonetheless, this effect may be compensated by taking omega-3 supplements.

Fernando Gomez-Pinilla, a professor of neurosurgery and physiological science at the University of California, Los

Angeles, said that food is akin to pharmaceutical compounds that affect the brain. Sleep, diet, and exercise can all affect your mental function and brain health. Hence, changing your diet can also enhance your cognitive skills, counteract the effects of aging, and protect your brain against damage.

The omega-3 fatty acids contained in walnuts, kiwi, and salmon are effective in improving memory and enhancing learning abilities. They can also reduce your risk of mental health problems such as mood disorders, dementia, depression, and schizophrenia.

Omega-3 fatty acids also support synaptic plasticity as well as positively influence the expression of molecules associated with memory and learning. These fatty acids are vital for normal brain development.

When you lack this nutrient, you can be at risk of attention-deficit disorder, dementia, bipolar disorder, schizophrenia, and dyslexia among other mental illnesses. It may also impair your memory and learning.

Coconut oil is another nutrient that is good for the brain. According to Dr. Mary Newport, a researcher, two tablespoons of coconut oil can provide you with twenty grams of medium-chain triglycerides, which can fight against degenerative neurological diseases.

Choline is also essential for your brain. It keeps the cell membranes in top shape and plays a significant role in nerve communications. It also prevents the accumulation of homocysteine in the blood and reduces the risk of chronic inflammation.

With proper diet, you can prevent brain injury and improve brain function.

Chapter 3: Apply Memorization Techniques to All Areas of Your Personal and Professional Life. Remember Names, Numbers, Lists, and Even Impress Your Friends

You have previously read about Ed Cooke, co-founder and CEO of Memrise, and his unusual expertise. According to his team, the following techniques can help you sharpen your memory:

Memrise Techniques

Be mindful of the location.

Context can mess with your memory severely. Say, you are in the kitchen when you suddenly thought of getting your coat from your bedroom. You go upstairs only to forget what you came there for. So, you head back downstairs and suddenly remember about the coat.

To prevent this from happening again, you should visualize what you are searching for in your chosen location. This way, your new context will hold the memory of what you need.

Train your brain.

Keep your brain active by acquiring new information constantly. You can read books, do crossword puzzles, learn a foreign language, and engage in intellectual conversations. See to it that your mind is always stimulated.

Play mind games.

Each memory is unique. Nevertheless, you can play certain games that are beneficial to the mind. For example, you can ask a friend to list down twenty words and ask you to reproduce them in exact order. Do your best to remember the words. Keep practicing until your brain becomes accustomed to this exercise.

Repeat.

As the saying goes, "repetition is key". Cooke conducted an online experiment that involved memory experts. They were asked to state the best techniques for memorization, and repetition was among their answers.

Words and simple concepts may have to be repeated up to thirty times before they stick. On the other hand, job presentations and speeches may require more repetitions since they are more complicated.

As much as possible, you should aim to comprehend the essence of whatever you are trying to memorize so that you can avoid making mistakes.

Tell a story.

The human brain is fond of stories. In fact, character-driven narratives can cause oxytocin to be released. This is the hormone that promotes empathy.

Stories have the characteristic of information that makes the brain remember and grow fond of it. This is why companies often use stories in their advertisements. They want people to remember their brands through the stories that they tell.

Other Effective Techniques You Can Use

The following are also highly recommended for improving your memory:

The Loci Technique

This ancient technique has been around for thousands of years. It originated in Ancient Greece and is also commonly referred to as "the memory palace".

In a study published in The American Physiological Society, it was found that 92.9% of the student participants were able to improve their information recall after three sixty-minute training sessions. The longer they practice the loci technique, the better their performance became.

The theory behind this technique is simple and straightforward. You must associate the things that you are trying to remember with specific images and places.

Ideally, you should choose a place with a personal significance, such as your bedroom or your favorite restaurant. This way, you will find the things inside them interesting and worth remembering.

The loci technique is effective in remembering information that has to be recalled but not processed, such as faces, names, lists, and birthdays.

Here is an example on how to use the loci technique or memory palace technique in everyday life:

1. Visualize yourself standing in your favorite place, such as your bedroom.

2. Mentally walk through your bedroom and notice any distinctive features that you can use to store the things that you want to remember. Every stop on your path would be a "loci". For instance, your bedroom door may

be the first loci and your bed the second loci. Remember these features so that when you think of this location, the objects and route in it will be ingrained in your memory.

3. Associate the things that you have to recall with the loci in your favorite location or "palace". Say, you have a grocery list. You can imagine coffee flooding your bedroom door and oatmeal cookies on your bed. Instead of seeing a nightstand, you can imagine an apple in its place. This may seem absurd, but it can actually make you remember your grocery list.

Mnemonics

This technique is popular among elementary students. When you were little, you may have used it to remember the months of the year or the correct order of the planets. Does "My Very Educated Mother Just Served Us Nine Pizzas" ring a bell to you?

In 2017, a study was conducted at the University of Florida. The researchers evaluated the effectiveness of mnemonics and learned that 71.2% of the student participants found it to be helpful in remembering and understanding study materials better.

Musical Mnemonics

These mnemonics are highly effective, especially in helping people remember and retain academic content, because they provide structure for information as well as encourage repetition.

People generally find it easier to recall catchy songs and tunes than to remember long strings of letters or words. This is the main reason why companies and even politicians use jingles to promote themselves and make their brands or messages stick.

For example, schoolchildren are taught the alphabet using the ABC song. Older students also sing the period table song to memorize the elements.

Expression Mnemonics or Acronyms

Just like when you used "My Very Educated Mother Just Served Us Nine Pizzas" to memorize the plants, you also probably used "Every Good Boy Does Fine" to memorize the lines of the treble clef (EGBDF) in music.

Likewise, you can remember the expression "looks the same, cooks the same" to remember chopping and dicing ingredients uniformly to cook food evenly.

Rhyming Mnemonics

These are similar to musical mnemonics, except that the ending of every line should rhyme. They create a pattern that is easy to recall. For example, there is a rhyme that helps you remember how many days every month has.

Rhyming Peg System

It is also referred to as the hook system. It is often used to memorize lists of items. For every number, you have to memorize a picture of the word that rhymes with it. This will give you a peg or hook for the things that you have to remember in order.

For example, if you have a list of grocery items and you have to remember them in order, you can use the following peg system:

1. Create or learn your rhyming peg, such as one bun, two shoe, three tree, etc.

2. Create a clear picture of the rhyming object of every number. In this example, you can visualize a bread bun, a running shoe, and a pine tree. Pay attention to their

details, such as the material of the shoe or the color of the leaves.

3. Imagine the rhyming object along with the item on your list. So, if your first item is hotdogs, you can imagine a hotdog sandwich. This is pretty simple since a hotdog in a bread bun is a pretty common sight. However, if your first item is milk, it can be quite ridiculous to imagine it being poured into a bread bun. Nonetheless, you should not hesitate to visualize these things, no matter how odd they may seem. You can visualize a milk container placed between bread buns. If your second item is chocolate chip cookies, you can imagine them being stored inside running shoes.

This technique requires quite a lot of creativity and effort. Nonetheless, it is very effective in helping people retain information longer as compared to when they try to merely memorize the words. Also, once you get used to your rhyming peg, you can use it for other lists in the future.

Chunking

This technique involves grouping things together so that they can be recalled easier and faster. It is ideal for memorizing social security IDs, bank account numbers, and phone numbers.

Its key aspect is grouping items according to semantic encoding. This means that things should be placed in groups based on pattern or context. For example, you may group your grocery list according to type or brand. Find a pattern that you are comfortable with.

If you want to learn a foreign language, you can sort vocabulary words by topic. You can also arrange list items according to their first letters or how many letters they have. You can also associate things with the larger group that they may belong to. For example, you can remember pizza = crust, cheese, sauce, pepperoni.

When it comes to memorizing numbers, such as phone numbers, you may group similar numbers together. For example, you can remember "000" "555" "7777" instead of "0005557777".

According to studies, the human brain is capable of holding four different things in its short-term or working memory. When you group data into smaller groups, you may hack the limits of your short-term or working memory so that you can remember more information.

This technique is effective because the human brain is designed to search for patterns and form connections.

The Building Technique

It may be built over the other techniques. It can also help people remember more data aside from simple facts, phone numbers, and names.

It is true that remembering facts is helpful. However, you need to have a profound understanding and deep knowledge of your profession or field of study as well.

A concept or fact that is fully understood has a greater chance of retaining in memory than something that is merely memorized. When you introduce meaning or a sense of understanding to the things that you want to remember, you can remember them better as well as apply them in various contexts.

Mind Maps

They are highly beneficial in improving creative thinking. However, they can also be used to learn new information and organize them more coherently.

A mind map has the elements of the building technique and the loci technique. It is effective in organizing huge, complex subjects into visual categories that are distinguishable. It can also break down multiple documents or long texts.

For example, if you just got hired, you can use mind maps to understand the products and/or services that your company offers. You can also use this technique to create your own marketing and sales strategies.

You can find software programs for mind mapping online. However, you can also create your own. For example, you can use a pen and paper. Simply write down an idea or topic that you want to remember. Express it using one to two words. Then, you should connect it to sub-topics according to relevance.

Lifestyle Modifications and Improvements

Of course, your diet, exercise routine, and general lifestyle play a huge role in your mental wellness. A healthy lifestyle brings about positive long-term effects on memory.

Hence, you should ensure that you get sufficient amounts of rest and sleep. You should also exercise on a regular basis and have a balanced diet. Start moving around if you have always been sedentary. Physical movements enhance learning skills and protect the memory.

Researchers at Harvard Medical School conducted a study in which the participants did an hour of brisk walking twice a week for six months. After the study, it was found that the hippocampus of the participants increased in size. This is the area of the brain that is associated with learning and verbal memory.

According to the researchers, it is crucial to do challenging exercises to elevate the pulse. This increases blood flow to the brain and ensures that enough oxygen is transported.

Dormancy is also crucial for a good memory. Researchers from Germany and Boston conducted a study that showed how lack of sleep affects the ability to perform simple tasks such as name recall and face recognition.

The participants were divided into two groups. The ones that stayed awake all night performed poorly compared to the participants that slept for eight hours before doing their tasks. This proves that sleep is necessary for optimum brain function.

The brain resets during sleep. It clears out neuron build up at nighttime to let you wake up refreshed and relaxed.

A balanced diet is also necessary. As you know, what you eat can affect the way you think, talk, and behave. For example, foods that are high in cholesterol can cause heart diseases. Such cholesterol can also build up in the brain, causing blood flow restriction and insufficient oxygen supply.

Time Blocking and Stuff Offloading

To keep your brain healthy, you need to take a break once in a while. Rather than try to remember everything, you can automate certain tasks or data such as birthdays, to-do lists, and shopping lists.

You can use time blocking, which is about blocking off time on a calendar to allow the brain to quit thinking about tasks since the time to do them has already been allocated. This helps the brain concentrate on tasks that are much more important. See to it that you also track how much time you spend doing your tasks so that you can properly adjust your blocks.

The human brain is amazing. Neurons are able to store multiple memories at once. Your mental capacity is around 2.5 petabytes. Nonetheless, even though it is highly unlikely for your brain to get full, it is still much better for you to offload certain information to digital tools.

For example, you can use Evernote to create to-do lists and manage your tasks. Apps like this are effective in increasing productivity. You can find a variety of other similar tools online. Download and use the ones that best fit your needs.

The above mentioned techniques are highly recommended by scientists. Although there are still a lot of mysteries that surround the human brain, these techniques will surely help you sharpen your memory and attain your goals.

Chapter 4: By Memorizing a Pack of Playing Cards

Is it possible to memorize a deck of playing cards in less than a minute? This may sound absurd, but the answer to this question is an astounding 'yes'. Even if you do not have a photographic memory, you can train yourself to have it.

Ed Cooke was, in fact, the Grand Master of Memory. When he was twenty-three years old, he memorized the order of ten decks of cards in sixty minutes and a shuffled deck of cards in just forty-three seconds. He also memorized one thousand random digits in sixty minutes and the order of a deck of cards in less than a couple of minutes.

Even better, he helped Joshua Foer, a journalist, to become Memory Champion in just one year. Foer memorized 120 random digits in five minutes as well as a shuffled deck of cards in over a minute. He also memorized the names of more than one hundred strangers in fifteen minutes.

What can you get from memorizing a deck of playing cards, you say? Aside from sharpening your memory and impressing a ton of people, you also get the chance to win thousands of dollars in competitions. This is a pretty good deal.

The Bicycleshop

This is the method Cooke used to memorize the playing cards. It is a combination of Photoshop and the playing card brand. It has two versions: Bicycleshop Lite and Bicycleshop Pro.

Bicycleshop Lite

It lets you memorize the playing cards as well as their order.

Step 1: Learn the cards.

You need to convert the fifty-two playing cards into fifty-two celebrities. As you know, the human brain does not remember the mundane. So, you need to give it something unusual in order for the information to stick.

As much as possible, you should attach a personality type and a profession to every card. This way, you will have two cues for every celebrity. Here is an example:

Spade cards – weird or amusing individuals

Club cards – tough individuals

Heart cards – lovable individuals

Diamond cards – wealthy individuals

The Playing Cards

You can associate these cards with professions. Odd numbers can be male while even numbers can be female. Pair up these cards. Then, remember that they represent powerful individuals. For example, 10's are powerful women while 9's are powerful men.

In order to facilitate such association, you have to include mnemonics below every profession. For example, the Queen can be the female half of celebrity couples while the King is the male half. This is relevant since celebrity couples are treated like royalty, anyway.

Jacks can represent religious figures and bachelors. 10 and 9 are the highest numbers. So, it is only fitting that they are used to represent the highest-powered individuals.

8s can be popular female physiques and 7s can be popular male physiques. Think of ripped or busty individuals. 6s can be controversial females while 5s are controversial males. After all, the number six sounds a lot like the word sex.

4s can be movie actresses and 3s can be movie actors. You can think of the movie trilogies. Finally, 2s can be female athletes and aces can be male athletes. Ace is often associated with sports excellence. You can also think of 2 as the "deuce" used in tennis.

Putting Everything Together

Now that you have selected four personalities and thirteen professions, you already have seventeen things to remember. You can use your current opinions and knowledge to fill in your 52-card matrix.

For example, you can think of the ace of diamonds as a man who became rich. Ace is associated with men while diamonds are associated with wealth. Your ace of diamonds can be Michael Jordan.

Then, the jack of spades can be an amusing religious figure. This can be the Dalai Lama, who is humorous and clever. The six of spades can be a controversial woman, such as Lady Gaga.

Through this method, you can fill out your matrix in less than one hour and successfully remember the individuals that represent the fifty-two playing cards. You can also shuffle your deck of cards and translate them to their images. Do not stop until everything sticks to your memory and becomes automatic. It may take an hour for you to do this. When you are done, you can arrange them in order.

Step 2: Memorize the order of the shuffled deck of cards.

You can now peg fifty-two cards to familiar locations. This can be a path from your driveway to your favorite café or a short distance from your bedroom to the garden. Choose whatever feels comfortable for you.

Some memory experts visualize their childhood homes. For instance, Scott Hogwood, U.S. Memory Champion from 2001 to 2004, used rooms from Architectural Digest luxury homes. When you use this method, you may position yourself mentally at the front door of every room. Then, you can move from where you are to the left and right corners, and eventually to the ceiling.

It only takes half an hour to select fifty-two locations. Then, you may begin positioning the celebrities at every point. At first, you can keep things simple. As you go on, you can use longer and more complicated paths.

So, for example, you can think of the Dalai Lama as the Jack of Spades. Visualize him standing at your front door, which is your first point. Then, visualize him at your second point, and so on.

Pay close attention to the details of the images in your head. Once you reach the end of your route, you should trace it back in your imagination. You should be able to remember every individual in your imagined sequence. You may have to go over this sequence two to three times before it sticks to your memory.

Bicycleshop Pro

This is an upgraded version of the Bicycleshop Lite. It is ideal for people who want to use a more effective compression algorithm. This method builds on top of the things that you already know.

With Bicycleshop Lite, you used fifty-two images. With this version, you can simply use seventeen to eighteen images so that you can memorize things much faster.

Still using the celebrities you assigned to the cards, you can associate them with a particular object and action.

For example, you can visualize the Dalai Lama praying and Michael Jordan playing basketball. The object associated with the Dalai Lama is the Buddha while the action associated with him is praying. The object associated with Michael Jordan is basketball while the action associated with him is dunking.

When you add this syntactic structure, your combination of cards can form short sentences that involve the celebrity from the first card, the action from the second card, and the object from the third card.

Using these methods require time and effort. You have to practice them several times until you get used to them. Don't worry because your efforts will not turn out to be futile. These methods are guaranteed to help you remember and memorize various things.

Chapter 5: Discover the Secret of the Oldest Memory Trick that Dates Back to Around 500 B.C.

You have read about the Loci Method, also referred to as the Method of Loci, in a previous chapter. This memory improvement technique is actually the oldest, dating back to the days of the Roman Empire.

The Method of Loci

"Loci," a word that is actually the plural of locus, refers to place or location. So, this technique is founded on the supposition that familiar places are the easiest to remember. When you associate something with a location or place that you know by heart, you can use this location or place as your clue to recall the information.

The loci method is a unique linking strategy. Simonides of Ceos, a poet who became the sole survivor of a tragedy, developed this method as attributed by Cicero.

Ceos was attending a banquet in Thessaly with several other people when their building collapsed. Although it was hard to identify the victims due to their conditions, he identified them by recalling where they were seated. This experience made him realize that it is possible to recall anything simply by correlating it with mental images of placements.

Greek and Roman orators also used this method to give public speeches without using notes. This technique gained intense popularity from 500 B.C. to the mid-1600s. It is best for people who have excellent visualizing skills.

How to Use the Method of Loci

Here are the steps on how to use this ancient method of remembering information:

Step 1: Picture a location or place that you know really well.

This can be anywhere, such as your home or office. Visualize certain paths in this location in a logical manner.

For example, you can visualize the route that you usually take to go from your bedroom to your backyard. Start at your bedroom door, walk down the hall, head to the kitchen, get out of the back door, and finally go to the backyard.

As you go through each location, you have to move consistently and logically in a single direction. You can also consider appliances and furniture pieces as additional locations.

Step 2: Put every object that you want to recall in every location.

Whenever you want to remember these things, you can simply imagine your home and go to every room in it. Every object that you associated a certain place inside your home must come into your mind as you imagine yourself going to each and every one of these places.

Say, you want to remember these items on your grocery list: toothpaste, deodorant, mustard, bread, and eggs.

As you imagine your home, you should also imagine toothpaste all over your front door. Do not just visualize the word "toothpaste". You have to really see the object in your mind. Imagine yourself pressing the tube and letting the toothpaste squeeze out of it. Recall the taste, smell, and feel of the toothpaste too.

Next, imagine yourself entering through the front door and walking down the hall to see a huge deodorant walking towards you. Imagine yourself walking past it to go to the living room. Here, you see a tall bottle of mustard dancing. Its yellow color is so bright; it's almost blinding.

You go to the kitchen to see a bread bun sitting while it stares at a fat egg wearing an apron. It goes to a frying pan to crack and cook itself.

Once you have visually positioned every item around your home, it would be easier for you to recall your grocery list. Simply imagine your front door. Your subconscious mind will immediately associate it with the toothpaste. Then, imagine your hallway to remember deodorant, and so on.

Do not hesitate to unleash your creativity. Be as outrageous as you can. The more interesting and absurd your mental pictures are, the easier it would be for you to recall them accurately.

The method of loci is not only effective in helping you remember lists. It is also useful in remembering important parts of speeches, names of people, tasks you have to do, and ideas that you want to share or turn into a project.

This method is very effective because it alters the way the mind remembers things. It involves the use of familiar places to give you cues about specific things. Since these places are organized in a manner that you are familiar with, every memory flows smoothly to the next.

You may also adapt this method by including buildings and other structures that you are familiar with. For example, you can visualize a church, mall, your best friend's house, etc.

It does not really matter how far or close apart every place is. The only thing that matters is how distinct they are from one another. With this being said, you may want to avoid picturing the library in your mind since it has identical aisles and shelves, and this might only confuse you. The places you visualize should be unique, memorable, and distinct.

You may also put several items in one location. For example, if you have fifty items on your grocery list, you can imagine five items in one location and another set of five items in the next location, and so on.

The Method of Loci In Modern Times

Although ancient, the method of loci is still useful today. In fact, it is widely used in contemporary memory competitions, such as the United States Memory Championship and the World Memory Championship. These competitions require memorizing sequences of numbers, letters, and playing cards.

Some of the most notable individuals who used the method of loci include Dominic O'Brien, Clemens Mayer, and Simon

Reinhard. This technique is also taught as a metacognitive strategy in learning-to-learn courses. It is used to encode the main ideas of a particular subject.

Chapter 6: Powerful Memory Techniques and Memory Skills to Increase Brain Function

By now, you should already know that brain health is significantly affected by diet and lifestyle. Aside from using accelerated learning techniques, you should also get adequate nutrition.

The way you eat and behave contributes to your cognitive decline. Hence, you should ensure that you get sufficient amounts of rest and sleep, a balanced diet, and a stress-free environment.

Moreover, a healthy lifestyle supports brain health and promotes neurogenesis or the process that involves growing new neurons. The hippocampus or the memory center of the brain is capable of producing new cells. It actually regenerates your whole life. So, even in your old age, your brain can still produce new neurons, as long as you keep it in top shape.

The following are some of the things you can do to learn faster, improve your brain function, and keep your brain healthy:

Exercise

You know how important exercise is. It stimulates the nerve cells to multiply so that your brain can work at its optimum capacity. It also strengthens the interconnections of nerve cells as well as protects them against damage.

When you exercise, your nerve cells release neurotrophic factors, which are proteins. The brain-derived neurotrophic factor triggers chemicals that lead to neural health.

In 2010, a study on primates was published in Neuroscience. It showed that regular exercise improves blood flow to the brain and promotes learning. These findings are also applicable to humans. In another study, it was found that those who exercised on a regular basis were able to grow and expand their memory center up to two percent annually.

Get Enough Sleep

According to researchers at Harvard University, people are thirty-three percent more likely to deduce connections among ideas that are not closely related after they have slept. However, only a few of them notice the improvements in their performance.

Sleep can enhance your memory. It can also help you practice your skills in order to improve them further. Simply getting four to six hours of sleep is already enough to influence your abilities to think clearly.

Neuroplasticity is said to underlie the capacity of the brain to manage behaviors, including memory and learning. Plasticity happens when the neurons get stimulated by information or events from external sources. Nonetheless, sleep loss and sleep alter the expressions of certain genes that might be necessary for synaptic plasticity.

In addition, some types of long term potentiation that are connected to the laying down of memory and learning may be elicited in sleep. This suggests that synaptic connections get stronger when you sleep. Even an afternoon nap can significantly restore and boost your brainpower.

Play Brain Games

When you do not challenge your brain, it starts to deteriorate. So, in order to keep your brain in top shape, you have to provide it with the right stimulus. For instance, you can play brain games.

There are lots of games available for brain training, particularly on the Internet. Websites such as Lumosity.com, for example, is a great source. Brain HQ is another ideal website with various brain exercises. They allow users to monitor and track their progress.

Dr. Michael Merzenich, a professor at the University of California, pioneered brain plasticity research. He also created a computer-based program to train the brain. This can sharpen your skills, from memorization to reading and comprehension.

Ideally, you should spend at least twenty minutes per day on brain games but you should not spend more than seven minutes on one task. The benefits of brain games tend to weaken when they are overdone.

Dr. Merzenich said that primary benefits are observed within the first six minutes of performing the task. Then again, if you are too busy, playing brain games may seem like an additional task rather than a new hobby.

Master New Skills

The neurological system gets stimulated when you engage in meaningful and purposeful activities. Likewise, these activities also counter the effects of diseases that are related to stress as well as reduce the risk of dementia. Choose tasks that attract your attention in order for them to be effective in boosting your brain health.

In one study, it was found that quilting, knitting, and other craft activities were connected to reduced chances of experiencing mild cognitive impairment. In another study, it was found that engaging in cognitively demanding activities such as taking digital photography improved the memory of older adults.

This technique would only be effective when you choose activities that stimulate you mentally. They should require your undivided attention as well as give you satisfaction. They should be activities that you are excited to do, such as painting, gardening, etc.

Intermittent Fasting

Ketones, not glucose, are fuel for the brain. They are fats that get mobilized by the body when carbohydrates are no longer consumed. This is why you have to consume healthy fats such as coconut oil.

Fasting for one day is enough to reset itself and burn fats instead of sugar. Moreover, it can reduce your total consumption of calories. This can promote the growth of brain cells.

As much as possible, you should restrict your eating schedule to a six- to eight-hour window. This would allow you to fast for sixteen to eighteen hours per day.

Chapter 7: Protect Your Memory from Deteriorating Due to the Aging Process

When you reach fifty years of age, you may notice certain changes in your body, including a decline in memory. Although memory lapses may occur at any age, they tend to occur more often with aging. They are typically caused by neurological illness, brain injuries, and organic disorders.

According to researchers, you may reduce your risk of dementia and prevent cognitive decline by living a healthy lifestyle. They especially recommend the Mediterranean diet, which involves vegetables, fruits, healthy fats, and whole grains.

Dr. Argye Hillis, a neurology professor at John Hopkins Medicine, said that you should refrain from eating red meats. In one study, it was found that those who followed this diet were twenty percent less likely to develop memory and thinking problems.

Most memory problems reflect natural brain changes, which may slow down the cognitive process and make it more difficult for you to process new information. Fortunately, there are a lot of things you can do to protect your memory from deteriorating.

Get treatment for pre-existing conditions.

Most of the medical issues that impair cognitive abilities are untreated or unrecognized. Hence, you need to get regular checkups to ensure that you are in excellent health. In case you get diagnosed with an illness, see to it that you have it treated right away.

For example, if you have diabetes, you have to follow your doctor's orders to treat your condition. Blood surges can hamper your memory by decreasing the supply of blood to your brain.

You should also manage your blood pressure since memory lapses can be caused by hypertension. In a study published in Neurology in 2009, it was found that the rate of memory issues increased by seven percent for every ten-point rise in diastolic blood pressure.

Researchers have also found that individuals with sleep apnea tend to score worse on cognitive and memory tests. However, when they keep their airways open as they sleep, they are able to get better scores.

Moreover, cognitive problems may be symptoms of depression. Women are especially prone to this mental problem. Their skills tend to decline quickly and they become more prone to developing Alzheimer's disease.

Don't forget to have your thyroid levels checked. Take note that hypothyroidism may affect memory, attention, and learning. With proper treatment, a better cognitive performance can be achieved.

You should also watch your cholesterol levels. High cholesterol levels can increase your risk of Alzheimer's disease and cognitive impairment. In a 2008 study, it was found that memory decline and low HDL levels are related to each other.

Take a memory course.

As much as possible, you should take a memory course that is run by experts in cognitive rehabilitation or psychology. See to it that it also focuses on the practical methods of managing daily challenges. Avoid courses that focus on concentration or computer games since they are not very helpful in real-world scenarios.

Keep your social life active.

Book clubs and other organizations are great because they keep you socially connected to other people. This helps your brain stay active. The more connections you have, the better you can preserve your memory and mental function.

Additionally, social interactions can boost your mood. This can help you prevent depression, which is a common cause of dementia.

Manage stress properly.

Stressors will always be around. You cannot magically make stress disappear from your life. As you grow, you encounter people, situations, and other factors that can make you stressed. When your body releases too much cortisol, you may find it hard to recall information.

This is why you should find time to relax and refresh once in a while. You can go to a spa and get a massage. You can also soak yourself in a hot tub. You can also try yoga and meditation. Whatever you do, make sure that it relaxes your mind and body.

Use memory tactics.

Each time you learn a new word or name, you can repeat it loudly so that it gets stuck in your memory. You can also mentally connect new words or names with images. For example, if you get introduced to someone named June, you can imagine a woman in a wedding dress to represent the month of June. You can also post sticky notes all over your office and home. You can also set reminders on your phone as well as mark your calendars to remember vital details.

Conclusion

I'd like to thank you and congratulate you for transiting my lines from start to finish.

I hope this book was able to help you learn about the different strategies you can use to improve your memory.

Having a sharp memory is beneficial to the different aspects of your life, including your personal relationships, health, finances, business, and career. It will not only impress your family members and friends, but it will also keep your brain in top shape.

In addition, it will prevent you from being embarrassed during social gatherings when you see someone you know by face but has forgotten their name. Having a sharp memory can also save your life since you can avoid making the same mistakes.

This book is all about sharpening the memory in order to learn faster and be more productive. It also discusses how certain factors, such as poor nutrition, can directly affect the brain.

It is also about training the brain to develop a long-term working memory. It will teach you how to remember lists, series of numbers, names, and even a deck of playing cards. Moreover, it is about conditioning yourself to become a memory master as well as to keep your brain healthy even in old age.

I hope that you follow the tips and recommendations stated in this book. Not everyone has a sharp memory. You are fortunate to find this book and get a chance to improve your memory.

The next step is to apply the lessons that you have learned into your life.

I wish you the best of luck!

Thanks for Reading

What did you think of, **Accelerated Learning & Memory Improvement To Learn Faster, Improve Your Memory & Save Time Even If You Have a Bad Memory Or Are Easily Distracted**

I know you could have picked any number of books to read, but you picked this book and for that I am extremely grateful. I hope that it added at value and quality to your everyday life. If so, it would be really nice if you could share this book with your friends and family by posting to Facebook and Twitter.

If you enjoyed this book and found some benefit in reading this, I'd like to hear from you and hope that you could take some time to post a review. I want you, the reader, to know that your review is very important and so, if you'd like to leave a review, all you have to do is click here and away you go. I wish you all the best in your future success!

Thank you and good luck

Trustgenics

The 11 Craziest Predictions About the Future Experts Say Are Going to Happen

Here are 11 predictions about the future that may surprise or even shock you—but one thing is certain: They're backed by some pretty smart people.

Find Out Now

www.ingramcontent.com/pod-product-compliance
Lightning Source LLC
Chambersburg PA
CBHW021102080526
44587CB00010B/350